NASA
SPACE SHUTTLE

H.R. SIEPMANN & D.J. SHAYLER

LONDON

IAN ALLAN LTD

629.441

United States distribution by

Motorbooks International
Publishers & Wholesalers Inc
Osceola, Wisconsin 54020, USA ®

Dedication

The first draft of this book was completed just one month before the *Challenger* disaster of 28 January 1986. Following that tragedy the text was revised to take account of the early findings of the crash investigation. The authors believe that the finest memorial to *Challenger's* gallant crew is the Space Transportation System itself, the basic building blocks of which are courage, vision and ingenuity, the finest human qualities.

This book is dedicated to the proud memory of the *Challenger* spacecraft and her fallen crew:

Mission Commander Francis R. (Dick) Scobee
Mission Pilot Michael J. Smith
Mission Specialist Judith A. Resnik
Mission Specialist Ronald E. McNair
Mission Specialist Ellison S. Onizuka
Payload Specialist Sharon (Christa) McAuliffe
Payload Specialist Gregory B. Jarvis

Acknowledgements

The authors would like to thank the many individuals and organisations whose assistance enabled this book to be written, and in particular: Lee Seagesser (NASA HQ); Lisa Vazquez (Johnson Spaceflight Center); Norma Kersman (Johnson Spaceflight Center); David Hollingsworth (UK Civil Aviation Authority), and Tim Furniss (spaceflight journalist).

CONTENTS

First published 1987

ISBN 0 7110 1681 X

Published by Ian Allan Ltd, Shepperton, Surrey; and printed by Ian Allan Printing Ltd at their works at Coombelands in Runnymede, England

3-88 BT 2200

PREFACE

There is no such thing as a typical Space Shuttle flight. The intention of this book is to present a wide view of the type of activities performed in the first phase of Space Transportation System operations (the first five years). To concentrate on the story of one real mission would not accomplish this, as each flight is unique. The book has therefore been written around an imaginary flight of the Orbiter which can be considered to have taken place at some time during the fifth year of STS operations. Although the flight itself is imaginary, the incidents are largely those which really occurred during a selection of missions, and the words of the crew are derived from genuine NASA voice tapes.

The photographs and illustrations which accompany the text have been kindly provided by NASA.

GLOSSARY

Access Arm Walkway connecting Launch Tower with Orbiter when on pad.

Aft Crew Station Rear area of upper deck from which vehicle is controlled during 'Prox Ops'.

Apogee The point of an orbit most distant from the Earth.

APU Auxiliary Power Unit.

Attitude The positioning of a vehicle in relation to its line of flight.

Attitude Control Thruster Reaction jet controlling attitude.

Auto Sequence The final part of a launch count-down, computer-controlled.

Built-in Hold A scheduled gap in a count-down, used to deal with unexpected or flexibly-timed events.

CAPCOM Capsule (or 'Spacecraft') Communicator.

Cargo Bay Synonym for payload bay.

CNES Centre Nationale d' Études Spatiales (French Space Agency).

Constant Wear Garment Light, close-fitting overall, the basic item of Shuttle clothing.

Control Surface Movable area of wing or fin which controls attitude by exerting an aerodynamic force during atmospheric flight.

Count-Down The final stage of a launch schedule.

Crawler Giant tracked vehicle used to transport Shuttle on its Mobile Launch Platform.

Crew Access Arm See Access Arm.

CRT Cathode Ray Tube.

DAP Digital Auto-Pilot.

EMU Extra-Vehicular Mobility Unit (space suit).

ESA European Space Agency.

ET External (Fuel) Tank.

EVA Extra Vehicular Activity (Spacewalks).

EV1, EV2 Designation of spacewalkers for identification purposes.

Fixed Service Structure Immobile part of launch tower.

Flight Coveralls Lightweight flightsuit.

Flight Crew Commander, Pilot and Flight Engineer (Mission Specialist).

Flight Deck Cockpit area of upper deck.

Frisbee Launch of satellite by 'rolling' it out of payload bay.

Fly Swatter Improvised device for remotely tripping a switch.

Geo Orbit Geosynchronous or 'stationary' orbit which occurs at 22,300 miles.

GLS Ground Launch System.

G Suit A garment which prevents pooling of blood under gravitational force by applying pressure to lower body.

Hold Pause in count-down sequence.

IMU Inertial Measurement Unit (a navigational device).

IUS Inertial Upper Stage.

JSC Lyndon B. Johnson Spaceflight Center, Houston, Texas.

knot One nautical mile per hour.

KSC Kennedy Spaceflight Center, Cape Canaveral, Forida.

Launch Control Controlling agency at KSC which controls countdown, launch and first moments of flight.

Launch Tower Servicing gantry consisting of Fixed and Mobile Launch Structures.

LDEF Long Duration Exposure Facility (a satellite).

LEO Low Earth Orbit.

LH2 Liquid Hydrogen.

LOX Liquid Oxygen.

Mach The ratio of the speed of a vehicle to the speed of sound in air at the same altitude, temperature and atmospheric pressure.

Mid Deck Crew compartment below upper deck.

Mission Control Agency at JSC which controls flight from Tower clearance to landing.

MMS Multimission Modular Spacecraft (a satellite).

MMU Manned Manoeuvering Unit.

Mobile Launch Platform Transportable structure on which Orbiter, ET and SRBs are mated and launched.

MSE Manned Spaceflight Engineer (A USAF grade).

NASA National Aeronautics & Space Administration, formed in 1958 from National Advisory Committee on Aeronautics (NACA).

Nautical Mile One minute of the Great Circle of the Earth. Equivalent to about 1.9km.

OMS Orbital Manoeuvering System.

OPF Orbiter Processing Facility.

O Ring Part of the seal between SRB segments.

PAM Payload Assist Module.

Payload Revenue-earning element of cargo.

Payload Bay (PLB) Cargo hold in which major items of cargo are carried.

PDP Plasma Diagnostic Package.

Perigee The point of an orbit closest to the Earth.

Pitch Movement of vehicle around a lateral axis in the vertical plane.

PLBD Payload bay doors.

PLSS Personal Life Support System.

Pressure Suit Spacesuit.

Prox Ops Proximity Operations; working a satellite which is in the immediate vicinity of the Shuttle.

RCS Reaction Control System.

Re-Entry Transition from space to atmospheric flight.

RSLS Redundant Set Launch Sequencer.

RMS Remote Manipulator System (Robot Arm).

Robot Arm See RMS.

Roll Movement of a vehicle about the longitudinal axis.

Rotating Service Structure Movable part of Launch Tower.

RTLSA Return to Launch Site Abort.

Snoopy Hat Fabric helmet containing communications equipment worn inside spacesuit helmet.

Sound Suppression System Water jets which deaden vibrations on pad at lift-off.

Spacelab Pressurised module, sometimes manned, carried in payload bay and used as a laboratory.

Spin Table Device for applying a rotational movement to a satellite before launch from payload bay.

SRB Solid Rocket Booster.

Stinger Device used on EVA to secure a free-flying satellite by inserting a capture probe into the rocket efflux nozzle.

T The theoretical moment of lift-off.

TDRS Tracking & Data Relay Satellite.

TPS Thermal Protection System (heatshield consisting of silica tiles, bricks and blankets).

Umbilical Connection via which oxygen, power and communication lines support a spacewalker (not used on Shuttle EVAs).

Upper Deck Upper area of crew compartment containing flightdeck and aft crew station.

VAB Vehicle Assembly Building.

Vandenberg US Air Force launch site in California where military and polar-orbit flights will originate.

Velocity Speed of a body in a given direction.

White Room Enclosure around entry hatch through which crew pass from Launch Tower to vehicle during count-down.

X-15 Pioneering single-seat rocket aircraft which provided much of the data on hypersonic flight which influenced Shuttle design.

Yaw Angular movement of a vehicle around its vertical axis.

Above:
Four crew members during training for Mission 61C prepare for simulated re-entry in the Shuttle simulator at Johnson Spaceflight Center. In the Commander's seat is Bob Gibson (right foreground) with Pilot Charles Bolden beside him. George Nelson (left) and Steve Hawley occupy MS seats at the rear. Note the launch/re-entry helmets with visors open, and the safety harnesses.

Discovery lifts off on its second mission. Exhaust clouds climb from each side of the pad through a deflection device used during Saturn moonshots. As *Discovery* clears the pad, control of the flight changes from the Cape to Mission Control in Houston, Texas.

ON THE LAUNCH PAD

In the crew quarters at Cape Canaveral the Commander of the Space Shuttle sits up in bed and rubs his eyes: it is launch day and the long months of training are about to pay off. NASA's aim is that Shuttle flights should ultimately seem as routine as airliner take-offs, but this is not the view of the men and women who ride the world's first reusable spacecraft: to them each mission is the climax of lengthy and arduous training during which their whole existence focusses on that weightless week of separation from the rest of humanity.

The Commander has flown in space before; he knows, in part, what to expect, but as a former jet fighter test pilot he has no illusions about the thin line that divides potential triumph and tragedy. His crew are mostly first-timers; every flight is different and somewhere along the Task/Time line the unpredicted will happen. That is when the experience of the Commander will be needed, to save a few pounds of fuel, or an expensive experiment, or the lives of everyone on board.

Now that the waiting is almost over he feels relaxed and ready. This is important, for a crew will always sense when a Commander is not at ease. He prepares for the pre-flight medical; after this final check of fitness the crew will gather for the traditional breakfast at which, no doubt, some old friends will be present to wish them well. Remembering the days of the Apollo moonshots the Commander is thankful that the tedious 'suiting-up' ordeal which used to follow breakfast has now all but

Below:
All Shuttle crews pose for a formal photograph before a mission, military and international personnel in parent service uniform or 'nationalised' dress. Sometimes there are other, unofficial portraits of a lighter nature; here the crew of Shuttle 14 celebrate a successful mission.

disappeared in the era of 'shirtsleeve' operations.

Outside in the flat, humid vastness of the Cape Kennedy Spaceflight Center, intense activity concentrates around the spacecraft which stands waiting on Launch Pad 39A. This too is the climax of effort which started months before, when the Orbiter returned to Earth from its previous mission. On that occasion, due to poor weather in Florida, it landed at Edwards Air Force Base in California and after post-flight inspection was ferried back to Cape Canaveral perched atop NASA's modified Boeing 747 Jumbo Jet.

Once home at Kennedy Spaceflight Center the Orbiter was stripped down, checked and refurbished in the Orbiter Processing Facility, which is capable of handling two Shuttles simultaneously. Some of the payloads for the impending mission were installed in the cargo bay whilst the vehicle was in the OPF. Then the spacecraft was moved to the nearby Vehicle Assembly Building, a structure famous since Apollo days when it was the largest building in the world. This huge workshop is so vast that, were it not for the air conditioning, clouds would form inside and rain would fall! Here the Shuttle was craned into a vertical position and mated with a brand new External Tank (eventually to be filled with fuel) and two Solid Rocket Boosters. These SRBs were assembled from parts which had already been launched on previous flights, recovered after being jettisoned into the sea, and refurbished for further use.

When the whole assembly was ready on its Mobile Launch Platform it was loaded on to a 3,000-ton tracked transporter called a Crawler (due to its 2mph top speed) and trundled to Launch Pad 39A. Here it was positioned beside the Fixed Service Structure, a scaffold-like gantry giving access to all parts of the spacecraft. A mobile Rotating Service Structure was then moved in to surround the Orbiter so that late payloads for the new mission could be installed in the vehicle's cargo bay.

Launch day has now dawned, and the countdown is already well advanced. It began a full two days ago, methodically working through many thousands of checks towards 'T', the moment of lift-off. At T minus 5 hours (when the crew was still asleep) a team of technicians and astronauts passed along the Crew Access Arm which joins the launch tower to the nose of the spacecraft and entered the Orbiter through a circular hatch one metre in diameter which opens on to the Shuttle's mid deck. The job of this Handover/Ingress Team is to make one last complete systems check inside the spacecraft before the final stage of the countdown may begin, thus allowing the flightcrew to come aboard.

The members of the Handover/Ingress Team report when they are satisfied that every switch is` set correctly and the ground communications network is established, and approximately 4½ hours before lift-off the ground support technicians start to fill the front section of the two-part External Tank (ET) with 143,000gal (541,255 litres) of liquid oxygen. This oxidant has a temperature of minus 297°F (minus 180.95°C) and weighs 1,359,383lb (616,500kg).

Approximately 45 minutes later the filling of the rear section of the ET with 385,002gal (1,457,233 litres) of liquid hydrogen begins. This fuel has a temperature of minus 423°F (minus 250.25°C) and weighs 224,910lb (102,000kg). Despite the supercold temperatures inside the tank its insulation is such that the outer surface stabilises around 0°F (minus 17.6°C).

By the time the Commander and his crew finish their breakfast things are really moving; the Shuttle stands on the pad in full view now that the enshrouding platforms of the Rotating Service Structure have been removed (at the completion of payload inspection on the previous day). Vapour from the volatile fuel drifts across the Launch Complex. The pad has been cleared, and the tanks of the sound suppression system are filled with a massive tonnage of water which, at lift-off, will spew from high-pressure jets across the launch pad to deaden the vibration of the thundering rockets.

With breakfast finished it is time for the astronauts to collect their flight gear and prepare for the ride out to the spacecraft. There is a strange feeling now; a kind of relaxed excitement and a knowledge that, in a sense, all attention is focussed on them. Everyone hopes that the launch will follow quickly, with none of the frustrating delays or even cancellations which have affected some previous missions. Launch is by no means the easiest part of the flight from an operational point of view. Because of this, and in particular to prevent deterioration in the alertness of flight crews at such a critical point, NASA doctors limit the launch pad waiting time of an astronaut to six hours. If the vehicle has not flown by the end of that time the launch will have to be 'scrubbed'. The two main enemies at this moment are the

weather and technical snags with the vehicle itself. A third, as today will demonstrate, is human fallibility.

The astronauts board the van which will take them to their spaceship. The ride to the pad is quite slow, with all the famous memories of Neil Armstrong and other legendary missions giving the short drive the atmosphere of a ritual. The crew members self-consciously wave to the cameras; they know they are about to make history, although in what context is still uncertain. Then it is time to board the elevator which will lift them to the platform on the launch tower from which they will cross, via the Access Arm, into the Orbiter itself.

The External Tank is now full and in 'Top-Off' mode. A one-hour 'Built-in-Hold' in the countdown is in progress to allow crew embarkation to proceed in an unhurried way.

In contrast to earlier days of spaceflight, when crews were encumbered by heavy spacesuits which hardly allowed them to walk, the Shuttle's crew wears little in the way of specialised clothing. The environment inside the Orbiter enables launch to take place with the astronauts wearing lightweight flight coveralls. A helmet and G-suit are the only concessions in the otherwise shirtsleeve

Above:
Ron McNair straps himself into his now horizontal seat on board *Challenger* during launch preparations for Shuttle 10 in 1984. He is seated behind Pilot Gibson and next to Mission Specialist Stewart. Two years later McNair was to lose his life in the same vehicle.

environment. (During the Shuttle test flights, when ejection seats were installed, pressure suits were worn for protection in the event of a high-altitude bail-out.)

Entering the Orbiter by crawling through the side hatch, the crew members move to their seats. The flightdeck is reached via an opening in its floor which, because the Shuttle is now standing on its tail, is on the right of the astronauts as they come aboard. This upper deck has seating for four including the Commander and Pilot. The rest of the crew is accommodated on the mid deck. (The Shuttle's maximum crew is seven, possibly eight, although on a rescue mission 10 occupants could be squeezed inside.) Sometimes there is only one mid deck occupant; the experience of sitting alone in that tight little compartment as chunks of red-hot insulation break off the ET and come thudding past the hatch window must be rather memorable.

Right:
Mid deck occupants have no outside view at launch; the only window is in the entry hatch. Here France's Patrick Baudry sports his launch/ entry helmet which provides oxygen in the event of a cabin depressurisation during the ascent or descent phases.

On the flightdeck the Commander and Pilot ease into their seats at the control console in front of the windscreen; the Commander sits on the left as in a conventional aircraft. In front of him an instrument panel stretches the width of the cockpit, dominated by three large cathode ray tube data displays. In the low centre of the panel is the keyboard for the all-important on-board computers and on a console between the two front seats are the digital autopilot controls. More instruments are set against the cockpit sidewalls including the cabin atmosphere regulators on the Commander's left and the auxiliary power unit controls on the right of the Pilot. Above the windscreen yet more switches and dials are clustered, governing further cabin atmosphere, engine and computer functions as well as radio equipment.

In comparison with the latest all-digital displays being developed for civil airliners (the so-called 'glass cockpits'), the Shuttle's flightdeck looks quite conservative, retaining the command-bars which give flight-attitude instructions to the Pilot by mechanical pointers, and which have been in use since the earliest days of navigational aids. Control of the vehicle is effected through stick and rudder-pedals as on a World War 1 biplane or a Boeing 707. Great effort has been put into making the Space Shuttle cockpit a place where a pilot will feel at home: it should be a place where his intuitive juices will flow freely, making his skill and experience as an aircraft pilot available in the spaceflight context.

One aspect of the scene, however, is definitely unlike an airliner: strapped in their seats, the astronauts are now effectively lying on their backs. Familiar Earth gravity pulls at them, but their eyes look up towards the blackness of space, which is separated from them only by a flimsy blue veil of atmosphere soon to be thrown aside.

A typical Shuttle crew consists of:

COMMANDER In overall command and the prime pilot for the manually-controlled phases of the flight.
PILOT More strictly a 'co-pilot', equally qualified as the Commander in flying the Shuttle.
MISSION SPECIALISTS Trained to operate the Shuttle's Mission equipment, such as the 'Robot Arm', to deploy satellites and conduct spacewalks.

PAYLOAD SPECIALISTS (These could include international personnel.) Responsible for the performance of a particular experiment or satellite.

OBSERVER A category which has become controversial since the Challenger tragedy: it was conceived as part of NASA's 'hearts and minds' programme aimed at giving spaceflight experience to individuals whose occupation would enable them to promote the Shuttle on their return to Earth (politicians, reporters, teachers, etc). In most cases Observers were considered to be Payload Specialists and had a particular function to perform within this category (for example Senator Jake Garn conducted a number of medical experiments in orbit). They also undertook passenger-assigned tasks such as food preparation and photography. Like astronauts they have to satisfy rigorous selection criteria: Garn, for example, was a former US Navy pilot with more flying hours in his logbook than any other US astronaut except Joe Engle!

As launch time approaches the busiest members of the crew are the Commander and Pilot, helped by one Mission Specialist who occupies a central seat behind them and acts as Flight Engineer. Cue cards are provided which may be attached to the instrument panel as 'prompts' for the long list of pre-flight checks, for despite the efforts of the Handover/Ingress Team there are still many systems to be tested before the launch can proceed. Radio communications, for example, comprise air-to-ground, air-to-air and intercom (crew-to-crew) channels. The air-to-ground channels link the Spacecraft with Mission Control, Houston, as well as Launch Control at the Cape. Failure of any one of these systems would cause cancellation of the lift-off.

The litany of checks now fills the radio circuits. The communication and telemetry links are confirmed as working; abort warning indicators are checked, then the groundcrew locks the entry hatch shut.

Launch Control 'Side hatch is secure.'
Commander 'Roger, hatch secure.'

The cabin atmosphere is checked for leaks and for correct pressurisation; all is well. The Inertial Measurement Unit (a navigation device) is tested, its indicator on the control panel in front of the Commander displaying the latitude and longitude co-ordinates of the launch pad. The computers are checked for correct programming. Eventually, with less than half an hour left before the scheduled

launch, the White Room surrounding the spacecraft's hatch is vacated and the ground-crew retire to a secure area at a safe distance from the pad.

Launch Control 'We now confirm groundcrew secure.'
Commander 'Roger, we copy groundcrew secure.'

Despite the extreme importance attached to the checklist, not all technical hitches discovered on the launch pad are of a critical nature, and the Shuttle's 'triple redundant' design (each system having at least two back-ups) enables it to fly with very minor faults corrected only by the selection of the appropriate back-up mode. This is a move towards standard airline operating procedure, the ultimate goal of the Space Transportation System. Nevertheless there are some systems which have a rating of 'Crit One' (Criticality One) which means that their failure could have fatal results. An example is the engine system; here any fault at all is considered major and will cancel the lift-off.

So far, on this mission, the countdown has progressed flawlessly; all systems are working well, the vehicle is almost ready to go. The astronauts wait in eager anticipation of the ride which will take them into space, and spaceflight history. One man is worried, however; he is the Range Safety Officer. Urgent messages are being passed. It seems that in spite of all the efforts NASA has made to warn shipping from the down-range area, a merchant vessel has strayed into the danger zone. It is now in the precise area where, shortly after launch, the jettisoned Solid Rocket Boosters will impact into the Atlantic. With such a potential hazard, the flight can not proceed; if the ship does not change course quickly a hold in the countdown will be necessary.

Someone makes a constructive suggestion: 'Get that guy out of there!' Despite the apparent good sense of this approach, care and diplomacy are needed: perhaps the ship is in trouble, or perhaps it is one of the Russian trawlers, packed with radio surveillance equipment, which frequently go fishing in that area at about launch time.

The situation is explained to the Commander, whose thoughts are no doubt explicit, but he limits his reply to a restrained 'Roger'.

At Launch Control fingers drum irritably on desks. On board the Space Shuttle on Pad 39A, as a steamer somewhere in the Atlantic turns hard about, the astronauts sit and wait.

LIFT-OFF...

The launch of Shuttle 20 turned night into day at the Cape. Night launches are governed by the need to deploy certain satellites at specific points in space at a given time during the flight.

If the offending ship can be cleared from the danger zone within a few minutes there is still a good chance that lift-off will be on time, as flexibility is built into the countdown. At T − 20 minutes there is a 10-minute built-in hold for dealing with unforeseen events or time slippages. Another such hold is available at T-9 minutes. If all is well the Launch Director will state 'Go for launch' at T − 9 minutes, and the Auto Sequence, the final stage of the countdown, will begin.

Aboard the spacecraft the Commander waits while, 125 miles to the east, the steamer leaves the SRB impact area. After a few minutes comes the message he wants to hear:

'Resuming the Count at T − 20 minutes'.

However, as if to remind the crew that there is still plenty of time for things to go wrong, Launch Control adds:

'We're watching the weather'.

On the flightdeck the Commander and Pilot are busy loading the flight plan software into the on-board computers. They are hoping silently that deteriorating weather (which has to be at least clear enough to permit pad photography) will not force another delay.

High level cloud cover and a belt of heavy rain approaching the launch site still threatens the lift-off. NASA weather watchers on the ground and in patrolling aircraft compare notes on the situation.

Launch Control 'T − 10 minutes and counting; we're going into the 9-minute hold very shortly'.

Aboard the Shuttle the Main Propulsion System Helium pressurisation is complete and all the Abort mode warning lights have been checked and found to be in order. The checklist is shrinking by the second.

At T − 9 minutes the last built-in hold begins. With the SRB impact area now clear the Supervisor of Range Operations gives a final 'Go for Launch', but the weather men are still not sure. At the end of a long 10 minutes it is time to make a judgement. Conditions have not worsened. There is a tense moment of hesitation in Launch Control; then the decision is made.

Launch Control 'We are GO for Launch!'
Applause breaks out amongst the relieved technicians.

At T − 9 minutes the Automatic Sequencer is activated and the computers take over control of the countdown.

Launch Control 'Have yourselves a super

mission, you guys; we'll see you back at the Cape next week'.
Commander 'We appreciate that'.

At T − 7 minutes 30 seconds the Crew Access Arm starts to retract. Should an emergency occur now the astronauts will not be able to evacuate the Orbiter until the White Room is put back in place round the entry hatch. Then they will exit through the hatch, pass as quickly as possible along the Access Arm, and mount a device resembling a ski-lift in which they will slide down wires to ground level. There an armoured vehicle (supposedly capable of surviving a launch pad explosion) will take them to the safety of a reinforced bunker.

Aboard the Shuttle the Auxiliary Power Unit 'pre-start' procedure is complete. Activation of the APUs will occur at T − 5 minutes to provide power for the spacecraft's hydraulic systems and enable the switch-over to internal power which allows further severance of the links between the vehicle and its servicing gantry.

Methodically the countdown progresses. It is now T − 5 minutes.

Commander 'We have three APUs up and running'.
Launch Control 'Copy that. Flightcrew close your visors'.

The astronauts seal the faceplates on their helmets as the final purge sequence of the main engines progresses. At T − 3 minutes 53 seconds the Shuttle's control surfaces are moved to a programmed pattern to establish correct function in the classic pre-takeoff check performed by pilots since the dawn of aviation.

Launch Control 'Go for ET LH2 pressurisation'.

On top of the vast External Tank the 'Beany Cap' retracts and swings out of the way, isolating the vehicle from ground loading equipment now that liquid hydrogen (LH2) replenishment has been terminated. With the LH2 Vent Valve closed and flight pressurisation underway, the voice of Launch Control dares to be optimistic.

Launch Control 'You are Go for launch; smooth sailing Baby!'

At T − 1 minute 20 seconds vapour billows across the launch pad as the main engines are purged ready for lift-off. Ten seconds later telemetry confirms that the Liquid Hydrogen tank is at flight pressure and all systems are 'Go'. At just after T − 1 minute the firing system for the sound suppression water is armed. The final minute ticks away.

With 30 seconds to go the Auto Sequence starts, shifting primary control of critical vehicle functions to the Shuttle's onboard computers. From now on the Ground Launch Sequencer serves only in support mode.

At T − 16 seconds the sound suppression system is fired, releasing tons of water across the launch pad. At the same moment computers arm the SRB ignition system.

Launch Control 'T minus ten, nine, eight . . .'

To a spacecraft commander 10 seconds is a long time. Previous missions have been aborted with just three seconds or less left in the countdown. Even after the main engines have fired they can be shut down by the Redundant Set Launch Sequencer without the vehicle leaving the pad. In this event Launch Control will announce 'We have an RSLS Abort', indicating that the main engines have been automatically cut off. In that case the Ground Launch System will be made safe immediately and after Launch Control announces 'GLS safing complete', a van will be sent to get the astronauts out. Of critical importance in such a situation will be the checks for fire indications or propellant leaks, especially as at this early stage the cause of the automatic abort is unlikely to be clear.

At T-8 seconds the three Space Shuttle main engines will fire in sequence by computer command. To onlookers the firing will appear to be simultaneous but in fact each engine ignites independently, the time gap between the firings being 120 milliseconds. At this point the Shuttle will still be secured to the launch pad, but the huge thrust of the rocket engines will nudge it forward in the direction of the ET. Until that moment the spacecraft leans slightly backwards, although this is hardly discernible to the naked eye.

The forward movement caused by the firing of the engines is known as the 'Twang', and it is of vital importance because precise timing is involved to ensure that the SRBs will ignite to launch the Shuttle at the exact moment at which the vehicle is vertically upright. (This twang was one of the aspects which received close scrutiny during the inquiry into the Challenger disaster. On the launch pad the entire weight of the Shuttle and its ET is supported by the Solid Rocket Boosters. The twang causes the joints between the cylindrical sections of each SRB to flex, a movement which their design accommodates. It was argued by some investigators, however, that small quantities of rainwater could have penetrated these joints and then turned to ice. Were this to happen, the integrity of the joint seals could possibly be threatened by the flexing motion.)

When the Space Shuttle main engines fire, computers will monitor the developing thrust. If at T-Zero any of the three main engines has failed to achieve 90% power a shutdown will automatically occur. It they are firing normally the SRBs will also ignite and the Shuttle will rise from the pad.

Now comes the moment familiar to TV viewers across the globe. The time-honoured words ring out almost like a ritual:

Launch Control 'Go for main engine start . . . Five, four, three . . . we have main engine start. Two. One . . . Solid Rocket Booster ignition and LIFT-OFF! We have lift-off of the Space Shuttle!'

At T, engine power is already at 90%. Two and a half seconds later, with the Shuttle vertical, the SRBs light. Once lit, they cannot be shut down whatever happens; therefore the Spacecraft is now committed to flight. The vehicle is released from the pad and climbout begins at T+3 seconds. It is the fastest climbing vehicle yet built to carry a human crew.

The next words which everybody wants to hear are:

'The Shuttle has cleared the Tower'.

As the spacecraft lunges upwards it comes to within 4ft of the retracted Access Arm, a minimal clearance which worried Chief Astronaut John Young on the first flight. As soon as this crucial clearance is achieved the Shuttle rolls 120° to the right and simultaneously pitches over slightly so that its climb is continued with the crew 'heads down' in an inverted position. This configuration has aerodynamic advantages.

With the launch completed, Mission Control at the Johnson Spaceflight Center, Houston, takes over from Kennedy Spaceflight Center to co-ordinate the remainder of the flight. The Commander's first call on the new frequency confirms good reception.

Commander 'Houston, we have a good Roll Programme'.
Mission Control 'Roger Roll'.

Ground communication is essential during the ascent phase and, as the Shuttle rapidly disappears over the horizon, radio messages are relayed through a series of stations down range. As a switchover approaches reception becomes weak; its quality is continuously

Left:
Here the start of the roll manoeuvre is visible as the Orbiter climbs away.

Below:
The sight no Shuttle Commander wants to see: this is the abort switch set at Abort to Orbit following an in-flight engine failure at the start of *Challenger's* eighth mission.

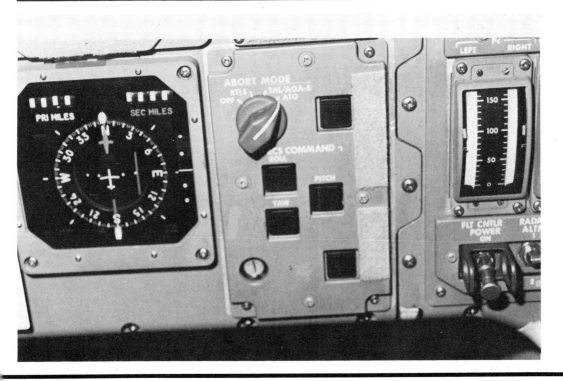

reported by the crew to Mission Control which informs the Commander 'Switching Bermuda', 'Going to Madrid in one minute' and so on throughout the climb.

With the Roll Programme complete the spacecraft is now climbing with the ET uppermost, and it remains thus for the rest of its atmospheric flight. Typically thrust is now at 104%; this is automatically reduced during the ascent to 65% by throttling down the main engines, in order not to exceed the 3G limit set for Shuttle operations. A limit of 3G has been set to reduce aerodynamic loads on the vehicle and to preserve an airliner-like cabin environment free of the excessive physical strains of earlier space vehicles.

The speed of the ascent is made possible by the Solid Rocket Boosters which use their thrust to counteract the deadweight of the External Tank. These SRBs are only needed for the first two minutes of flight, when the ET is full. At altitude, when the Shuttle has attained supersonic speed, the ET is lighter, its fuel being consumed at an astonishing rate and therefore the main engines can cope without further assistance. Never before in the history of manned spaceflight have solid propellant (unthrottleable) rockets been used as a main source of power. Another first is that the spent SRBs are parachuted to Earth for refurbishment and reuse on a later mission.

The early seconds of the climb are the most critical; with no ejection seats the crew's lives depend on the safe return of the whole ship. Failure of one SRB is not survivable, but if one of the main engines fails immediately after lift-off the Commander can attempt a Return to Launch Site Abort (RTLSA). In order to return to the runway at Kennedy Spaceflight Center it would first be necessary to turn the vehicle around through 180°. As much altitude as possible would therefore be needed to extend the flight-time and consequent range of the craft. The SRBs would remain attached until their fuel was exhausted; once burnt out they would be jettisoned, and every available source of thrust left aboard the Orbiter would be fired at maximum and a pitch manoeuvre would be initiated to turn the Shuttle around. This turnaround could take 36 seconds or more.

Once the fuel was exhausted, the ET would be jettisoned and, with luck, the vehicle would have enough height left for a glide return to the Cape. Although practised routinely in the simulator an RTLS Abort would be perhaps the severest test of flying skill yet devised in aviation.

If for some reason the turnaround was unsuccessful a ditching in the sea would be possible, as with any conventional aircraft. This should be survivable because the very large deceleration forces would be partially absorbed by the vehicle breaking in two along a design soft-point. The entire nose section containing the crew compartment would break away and hopefully would continue to float, at least long enough to enable the crew to exit via the overhead roof hatch and windows.

Shuttle flight crews train for all these possible situations using flight simulators, and also performing ditching drill 'for real' in the ocean.

The Commander checks the engine data on the displays; so far there seem to be no problems. Within the first minute of flight the spacecraft is at supersonic speed. As the climb continues the engines are gently throttled back up to 104% power and the vehicle approaches its maximum dynamic pressure ('Max Q').

Mission Control 'You are Go at throttle up'
Commander 'Roger, Go at throttle up'

Mission Control (Carefully watching the Shuttle trajectory) 'You are lofting a little bit; you'll probably be a little high at staging'.

'Staging' is a term which survives from the days of expendable launchers, when rockets consisted of a series of boosters mounted in a stack. These boosters were known as stages, the second stage igniting in flight when the first stage burned out and was jettisoned. In the Shuttle era the equivalent of staging is the burn-out and separation of the SRBs.

On the cathode ray tube (CRT) display in front of the Commander a signal indicates that the pressure in the SRB combustion chambers has fallen below 50lb/sq in. Although smoke and flame continue to trail from the booster nozzles, the rockets are now useless. At 2 minutes 12 seconds into the flight the Shuttle is at 31 miles altitude, flying at 4½ times the speed of sound (Mach 4.5). Mission Control monitors the situation.

Mission Control 'You are Go for SRB separation'.

Each SRB carries eight 'separation squibs', small rockets clustered in groups of four at the nose and tail of the SRB. Each squib has a thrust of 22.05lb (98.08N). As the SRBs burn out, pressure sensors detect the fall in thrust and trigger the squibs automatically. The two solid boosters detach from their mountings on the ET: still spewing fire, they arc away from the flightpath, gracefully curving into a free fall.

Commander 'There they go'.
Mission Control 'Roger on the sep'.

Ground cameras track the tumbling boosters as they descend towards the Atlantic. Then parachutes deploy as the cones are jettisoned. The SRBs slow to a safe speed and eventually splash into the ocean to await recovery by the support ships UTC *Liberty* and UTC *Freedom*. They will be returned for refurbishment and suitable parts will be prepared for a future flight.

The velocity of the Shuttle is now 5,100ft/sec (1,555m/sec). Its rate of climb is 1,400ft/sec (427m/sec) and it is 33 miles (53km) downrange. The onboard guidance is progressing according to plan and now another important milestone is reached.

Mission Control 'You have two-engine Transatlantic Abort Landing capability'.
Commander 'Roger two-engine TAL'.

If an engine fails now a Transatlantic Abort will be possible, the Shuttle descending to an emergency landing at Saragossa, Spain, (downrange from Kennedy Spaceflight Center), one of a network of similar landing grounds at strategic points around the world. This is necessary because the Transatlantic Abort is but one of the possible emergency landing options.

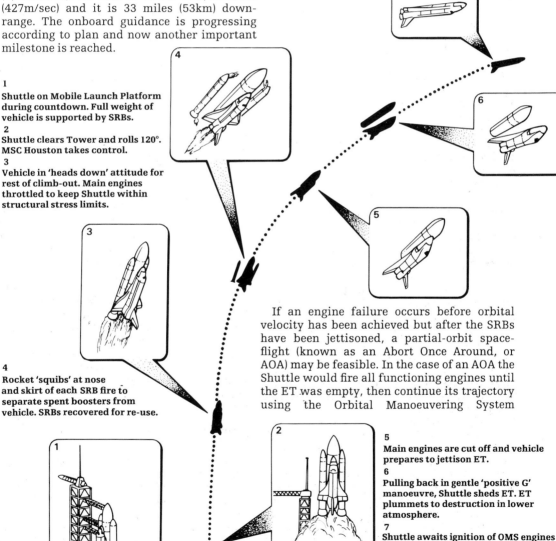

1
Shuttle on Mobile Launch Platform during countdown. Full weight of vehicle is supported by SRBs.
2
Shuttle clears Tower and rolls 120°. MSC Houston takes control.
3
Vehicle in 'heads down' attitude for rest of climb-out. Main engines throttled to keep Shuttle within structural stress limits.
4
Rocket 'squibs' at nose and skirt of each SRB fire to separate spent boosters from vehicle. SRBs recovered for re-use.

If an engine failure occurs before orbital velocity has been achieved but after the SRBs have been jettisoned, a partial-orbit spaceflight (known as an Abort Once Around, or AOA) may be feasible. In the case of an AOA the Shuttle would fire all functioning engines until the ET was empty, then continue its trajectory using the Orbital Manoeuvering System

5
Main engines are cut off and vehicle prepares to jettison ET.
6
Pulling back in gentle 'positive G' manoeuvre, Shuttle sheds ET. ET plummets to destruction in lower atmosphere.
7
Shuttle awaits ignition of OMS engines which provide final thrust for insertion into Earth orbit.

17

A discarded ET falls to destruction over the Indian Ocean eight minutes after the launch of Shuttle 20.

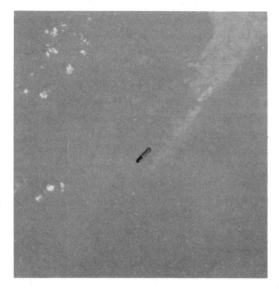

engines to lengthen the distance of flight. In theory it would be possible to travel the 20,000 miles to the emergency landing ground at Northrup Strip, White Sands, New Mexico, using this method. Alternative abort sites will increasingly become available.

Three minutes and 55 seconds of the flight have now elapsed.

Mission Control 'Standby press to MECO'.
Commander 'Roger, press to MECO'.

Main Engine Cut Off (MECO) will occur when the ET is empty. It will then be jettisoned to fall back into the lower atmosphere and burn up with the friction of re-entry. The Shuttle will then fire its smaller Orbital Manoeuvring System engines to achieve orbit. Should one or more of the main engines fail before the planned point of MECO is reached an Abort to Orbit (ATO) can now be attempted.

In the later stages of the climb the Shuttle achieves sufficient energy to reach orbit with double main engine failure. In this event unnecessary fuel can be dumped to lighten the vehicle. At any stage of the climb-out it is vital that the Commander be aware of the abort options available to him. Mission Control will therefore inform him, for example, when a Transatlantic Abort can be achieved on the power of two engines ('Two Engine TAL capability'); later, as energy increases, Mission Control announces 'Single engine TAL', indicating that only one engine is now necessary for this type of abort. When orbit can be achieved with two failed main engines Houston calls 'Single engine press to MECO'.

In the event of an Abort to Orbit (which first occurred on Shuttle 19) the power loss due to the failure of an SSME is balanced by a longer-than-normal burn of the Orbital Manoeuvring System engines, and once orbit has been achieved the mission may be able to continue more or less as planned.

More than four minutes have now elapsed since Lift-off.

Mission Control 'Standby for Negative Return; on my mark . . . (a short pause) . . . Mark! Negative Return'.

The Shuttle is now committed to completing the trip into space. As with a commercial airline flight, there is a point beyond which it is easier to go on than to turn back. Having passed this point the Shuttle needs just one main engine to keep working and the safety of orbit will be achieved.

Throttling is continued to keep the vehicle within the 3G limit as it hurtles towards space. By the time six minutes of flight have elapsed its speed has increased to Mach 15, and altitude is 80 miles.

The next major operation is Main Engine Cut-Off, to be followed 20 seconds later by separation of the External Tank. To ensure a clean separation the Shuttle must 'pull G' in much the same way as a military jet pulls G to toss its bombs from their racks.

Still flying inverted the Orbiter flattens its trajectory, passing into horizontal and then into slightly diving flight. G is held at the maximum of 3 and the spacecraft swoops eight miles towards the Earth.

Now the three main engines are shut down and the External Tank is released.

Commander 'ET Separation is good'.
Mission Control 'Roger ET Sep'.

The Shuttle carries out an evasive manoeuvre to avoid the danger of collision with the ET. The spent tank is visible through the Commander's window as it arcs downwards towards the ocean; its brown insulation is badly charred by the aerodynamic friction of the ascent and by the adjacent rocket exhausts. As its speed increases it will suffer further heating until its aluminium skin glows first red, then white hot. The tank remains in one piece until it has reached 165,000ft altitude, still in the upper atmosphere. Thereafter disintegration is rapid and the last of the debris spatters the Indian Ocean in a 'footprint' of 100 by 600 miles. The nearest land is more than 200 miles away and the area is free of shipping lanes.

On the Shuttle's first flight Commander John Young was surprised at the battered appearance of the ET as it fell away. 'It looked like it had been in a war', he said. The tanks on the first two flights were painted white. Later a new tank was developed. This incorporated structural improvements which reduced weight by 5,000lb (2,268kg). Leaving the tank unpainted, apart from a spray-on insulation, saves another 1,400lb (635kg).

The ET, although expensive to produce, is the only non-reusable part of the Space Transportation System; to make it recoverable would impose severe weight penalties and the cost of retrieval and refurbishment would be higher than the cost of building a new tank from scratch. (It has been suggested that NASA might extract some extra value from the spent ET. One proposal involved fitting the tank with its own booster rocket to enable it to achieve orbit. Once in space the Tank could be cut into sections to form the basic structure of space-station type vehicles. This concept was not new; Skylab, NASA's successful space-station of the 1970s, was made from the hollow shell of a rocket.)

With the ET successfully jettisoned, the Shuttle now looks ready for orbit. In fact there is still a major hurdle to be negotiated. To put the vehicle into space a final 'kick' is required, and for this the rockets of the Orbital Manoeuvering System (OMS) will be used. This final kick will be delivered in two separate stages.

The OMS comprises two rocket engines of 6,000lb thrust each. These are situated in the two large pods visible at the rear of the Shuttle. The pods house not only the OMS engines but also the aft Reaction Control System thrusters, which use the same fuel as the OMS.

In principle the OMS rockets are similar to the main engines, although much smaller. They give the Shuttle the final boost necessary to achieve orbit and, once in orbit, enable the Spacecraft to change altitude. Most Shuttle missions involve heights of around 100 miles, although a 690-mile maximum is possible.

The OMS engines are also used at the end of a flight; by firing them against the direction of travel the vehicle is slowed to below orbital speed and atmospheric re-entry results.

So far on this flight the OMS engines have not been used. They must work properly if the mission is to proceed. The first of the two consecutive burns is now imminent.

Mission Control 'You are Go for nominal OMS one; (the word is pronounced as 'ohms'). You are Go for APU Shutdown on time.'
Commander 'Roger that'.

The Commander enters the correct instruction on the panel of the Digital Autopilot, situated on the central console between the seats. The engines fire. After two minutes:

Commander 'We have OMS cut-off.'

So far, so good. Now the two small doors on the belly of the Orbiter through which the fuel was drawn from the ET must be closed. It is impossible for the crew to see these doors even by using remote TV cameras. Closure and secure latching are essential with the Shuttle on the threshold of space. Instruments confirm the success of the operation.

The first OMS burn has placed the spacecraft in a low elliptical trajectory which, in physical terms, amounts to a continuous free fall, the pull of the Earth's gravity being exactly balanced by the centrifugal force of the 17,500mph speed which the Shuttle has reached. This orbit will eventually decay, however, due to drag imposed by the upper vestiges of the planetary atmosphere. A second OMS burn will therefore be used to circularise the flightpath.

After 45 minutes the vehicle has travelled half-way round the world.

Commander 'Okay, looking good for OMS two.'
Mission Control 'Roger that; ready for OMS two.'
The second burn lasts for just over 2½ minutes. Then the Orbital Manoeuvering System is cut off.

Commander 'We had a good OMS two; vehicle checks were good and we're just starting the post-insertion (checklist).'
Mission Control 'We copy; looked good to us too.'

For the first time since lift-off none of the Shuttle's engines are firing; nor does the spacecraft need engine power to remain in flight. From now on the vehicle will be kept circling the Earth by the same natural forces that make the Moon go around the Earth and the Earth go around the Sun. For the Commander this represents a major plateau in flight safety, for the high workrate of the ascent is over. Now he has more time to make decisions and weigh up alternatives; and the real work of the mission can begin.

SHUTTLE ON ORBIT

The Shuttle is now in a circular orbit 190 miles (306km) above the Earth (NASA says 'on' rather than 'in' orbit). Before a 'Go' can be given to continue with the mission, vehicle checks must be carried out and the Payload Bay Doors opened. On the insides of these doors are radiators which shed the excess heat caused by solar radiation and the spacecraft's own internal systems. The doors are therefore opened as soon as possible after reaching orbit and remain open until the ship prepares for atmospheric re-entry. The maximum flight time permissible with the doors closed is eight hours.

From now on the Commander is as much a manager as a pilot. Flexibility exists during the mission to adapt the flight plan to circumstances. Fuel cell leakage, for example, has caused flights to be shortened while in contrast there have been cases when good housekeeping has enabled more to be achieved than was planned. One such case was

Above:
Using the Orbital Manoeuvring System (OMS) the crew refines the orbit of the Shuttle to the desired operational altitude. They also open the payload bay doors and check the Robot Arm (if carried) which is stored on the right side of the bay. With the payload bay doors opened the cargo is exposed to the vacuum of space; it is monitored by the flightcrew via telemetry. Also, sun shields are closed around satellites to protect them whilst they remain inert in the bay. Most missions spend the majority of orbital stay-time with the payload bay facing 'down' to Earth.

Shuttle 9/Spacelab 1, when John Young's frugal use of resources enabled an extra day to be flown. This kind of bonus can be welcome if landing sites are affected by bad weather.

At its orbital speed of 17,500mph (28,163km/hr) the Shuttle is now circling the globe approximately every 90 minutes. Because at any given time half the world is in darkness, the spacecraft passes from day to night and back to day again with each revolution. Time, therefore, must be given an alternative reference base to the day/night pattern used on Earth. 'Mission Elapsed Time', pegged on the time of lift-off, is used and the Shuttle crew follows the work/rest cycle of Mission Control, Houston. This prevents jet-lag from being added to the already common discomfort of Space Adaptation Syndrome — motion sickness.

Complex tasks such as Extra Vehicular Activity (EVA) would not normally be conducted on the first day of a mission unless there was some pressing reason, such as a rescue operation in which lives were at stake. Satellite launches, however, have now become routine enough to be included on the first day of the flight plan, just a few hours after achieving orbit.

The astronauts are now weightless and therefore their seats are no longer required. They are folded away, except for the Commander's and Pilot's fixed seats on the flightdeck. Preparations for the particular mission continue; for example, a further burn of the OMS may be necessary to close the gap with a target or to establish specific orbital parameters.

The Remote Manipulator System (RMS), often called the Robot Arm, must be uncradled and checked by the Mission Specialist assigned as Primary RMS Operator for the mission. Any faults in this system could have a critical effect on the success of the flight, especially as the Arm is not just a space-crane for satellites but a useful tool in the case of emergencies.

Payload Specialists, meanwhile, busy themselves with setting up or preparing for their particular experiments.

Mission Control 'You are Go for Payload Bay Door opening.'

The doors slowly open, allowing sunlight to flood in and reveal the equipment stowed in the bay. White screens shield the cargo from the fierce solar radiation.

Commander 'Roger, Houston, the Payload Bay Doors are open on nominal, and we're truckin' along.'

After further checks come the words the crew has been waiting for:

Mission Control 'You are Go for orbit ops.'
Commander 'Roger, understand Go for orbit ops; that's good news.'

In the payload bay, beneath sunshields, two satellites await launch. Telemetry monitors their condition. The sunshields can be opened and the satellites inspected visually or with TV cameras, and if necessary by a spacewalking astronaut; launch will not take place until these 'health checks' are complete.

In this case no problems are apparent, at least to the Commander. He reports when his checks are finished.

Commander 'All health checks are complete, the sunshields are closed and we have no anomalies to report.'
Mission Control 'We did see one: the solid rocket motor temp transducer failed off-scale high.'
Commander 'Okay; we don't look at that parameter. Thanks for the word.'

Fortunately the problem is a minor one which will not affect deployment of the satellite. Preparations for this operation continue.

The Shuttle is now approaching a loss of signal point, due to the curvature of the Earth, when communications will be cut off for a short while until the spacecraft is in range of the Hawaii relay station.

Mission Control 'We'll see you in Hawaii at five four. This is the Ascent Team signing off now. We'll talk to you in a few days about coming home.'

With the Shuttle safely in orbit the team of flight controllers at Houston is changed, so that when signal acquisition occurs over Hawaii a new voice will be heard from Mission Control. The Commander thanks the Ascent team for their help during the launch phase.

Commander 'See you down the road a little bit, you guys.'

As the ship circles the world it is tracked by NASA's NASCOM network. Up to 3,000 people operate this facility which is controlled from the Goddard Spaceflight Centre and is linked with 15 ground stations (in the USA, Australia, Botswana, Bermuda, Chile, England, Senegal and Spain). Much of the electronic data of a flight is relayed through the SATCOM system which has 10 Earth stations.

Small orbital changes during the mission are made by firing the Reaction Control System (RCS) and vernier jets housed at the nose and tail of the Orbiter. This view, taken during Shuttle 6 in 1983, shows a firing of a vertical aft jet.

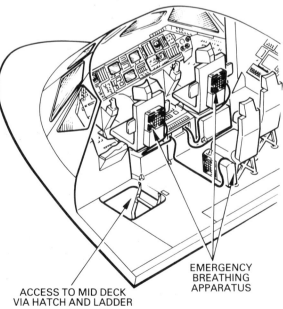

Right:
Seating layout on flightdeck in launch and re-entry configuration.

Facing page, bottom:
Flightdeck and mid-deck layout. Mission and payload specialists' seats are folded away in orbit.

ACCESS TO MID DECK VIA HATCH AND LADDER

EMERGENCY BREATHING APPARATUS

During the early days of the US Space Programme communication with the ground was very complex due to the speed with which low flying spacecraft disappear over the horizon and thus out of the 'line of sight' of radio signals. NASA had to establish a network of tracking stations, many of which were in remote areas, where communicators would sit anxiously awaiting the next five-minute contact.

The Space Transportation System is designed to replace much of this network with a pair of large satellites in geosynchronous orbit. Such an orbit occurs at an altitude of 22,300 miles (35,887km) when it takes a satellite 24 hours to complete one revolution of the globe. Since the Earth takes exactly the same period to revolve once on its axis, it follows that the satellite will remain always above the same point on the surface. It will never, therefore, disappear below the horizon.

Careful positioning of these satellites, called Tracking & Data Relay Satellites (TDRS, pronounced Teedras) should ensure that the Orbiter will be able to remain in contact with Mission Control for much longer periods than was possible in the Moonshot days. The second TDRS was part of the payload of *Challenger* on its last flight.

As well as the obvious voice-radio, communications with the ground include an onboard teleprinter (handling yards of print-out in weightlessness can be spectacular!), a direct ground-to-space link with the digital autopilot and numerous telemetry links which enable Houston to monitor onboard systems and even the medical condition (when necessary) of the crew. These facilities are all based on previous experience in earlier programmes and they enable problems to be discussed by specialists on the ground. Nevertheless, as on an airliner, the Commander has responsibility for mission safety and no actions will be taken without his agreement. This is in marked contrast with the Mercury and Gemini era when astronauts were sometimes instructed by Mission Control to take actions without even being told the reason.

The Shuttle, still in its 'heads down' position relative to the Earth, passes over Kennedy Spaceflight Centre as another orbit nears completion. The Commander, looking 'up' through the cockpit windows, can pick out the runways and the square shape of the Vehicle Assembly Building with the naked eye. Off the coast, ships' wakes are clearly visible.

But there is no time for sight-seeing. Although the Mission Specialists are now the focus of attention as the scientific work begins, the Commander and Pilot remain in primary control of the vehicle itself. With the all-important digital autopilot they have the responsibility of ensuring that the vehicle is in the right place at the right time.

Major changes in the Shuttle's position, such as a move to a new orbit, are achieved by using

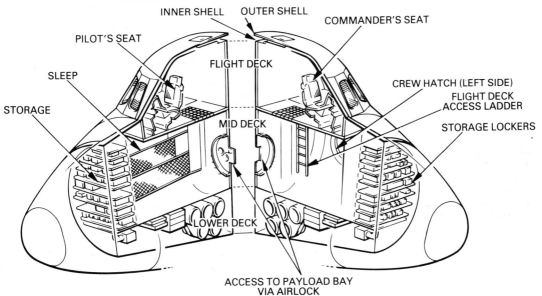

SELF-CONTAINED NOSE COMPARTMENT
ENCLOSED BY SEPARATE OUTER STRUCTURE

INNER SHELL   OUTER SHELL

COMMANDER'S SEAT

PILOT'S SEAT

FLIGHT DECK

SLEEP

CREW HATCH (LEFT SIDE)
FLIGHT DECK
ACCESS LADDER

STORAGE

MID DECK

STORAGE LOCKERS

LOWER DECK

ACCESS TO PAYLOAD BAY
VIA AIRLOCK

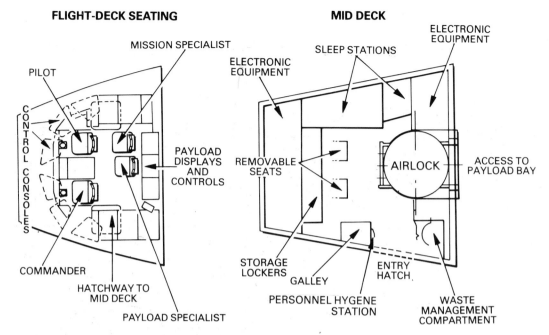

FLIGHT-DECK SEATING

MISSION SPECIALIST

PILOT

CONTROL CONSOLES

PAYLOAD
DISPLAYS
AND
CONTROLS

COMMANDER

HATCHWAY TO
MID DECK

PAYLOAD SPECIALIST

MID DECK

SLEEP STATIONS

ELECTRONIC
EQUIPMENT

ELECTRONIC
EQUIPMENT

REMOVABLE
SEATS

AIRLOCK

ACCESS TO
PAYLOAD BAY

STORAGE
LOCKERS

GALLEY

ENTRY
HATCH

PERSONNEL HYGENE
STATION

WASTE
MANAGEMENT
COMPARTMENT

the two OMS engines. Minor adjustments and general in-flight manoeuvres are achieved via the Attitude Control Thrusters of the Reaction Control System. These are situated on the nose of the vehicle in front of the flightdeck, and at the rear of the OMS pods. The thrusters use the same fuel as the larger OMS engines; a mixture of monomethyl hydrazine and, as an oxidant, nitrogen tetroxide.

An example of the importance of attitude orientation is provided by the mysterious glow first noticed on Shuttle 3. Surfaces which face in the direction of the Orbiter's flight accumulate a glowing orange layer thought to be caused by oxygen atoms and molecules interacting with the ship's skin. The glow can be bright enough to affect optical or light-sensitive experiments; it is therefore preferable that the Shuttle be positioned so that the experiments can be carried out away from the most intensely glowing area.

The Reaction Control System provides rotational and translational manoeuvre components using a combination of primary thrusters of 870lb thrust and 'vernier' thrusters of 24lb thrust for precise manoeuvre refinements. The RCS is designed to last for 100 flights or 50,000 firings.

The RCS thrusters can move the Shuttle in pitch, roll and yaw, so that any combination of movements can be carried out. They are operated from the flightdeck where two separate control stations are available. As well as the controls in front of the Commander's and Pilot's seats there are duplicates at the

rear of the cockpit in the Aft Crew Station. These are only used in orbit, therefore seats are not necessary. The astronauts stand facing two small windows which look aft into the payload bay. Two more windows in the roof increase visibility. From this position the Shuttle can be guided to within a few feet of a free-flying object, such as a satellite, with the pilot able to see the full length of the vehicle all the time.

Beside the RCS control position in the Aft Crew Station are the controls for the Remote Manipulator System, or Robot Arm. These move the Arm up, down or sideways and can also flex it about its 'shoulder', 'elbow' and 'wrist' joints. The combination of RMS movements and the Shuttle's precise manoeuvrability creates an almost unlimited range of capabilities.

Control of the RMS is a specialist function requiring much training and a Mission Specialist will be assigned to take overall charge of RMS operation on any mission.

Best friend of the flightcrew on orbit is the digital autopilot. The 'DAP' is really an electronic committee in which five computers (two are back-ups) debate complex problems at lightning speed. If they ever fail to agree they vote and give the Commander a truly democratic decision.

These computers have their own language, High-order Assembly Language (Shuttle) or 'HAL/S'. As well as a large bank of programs for standard flight plan tasks such as re-entry,

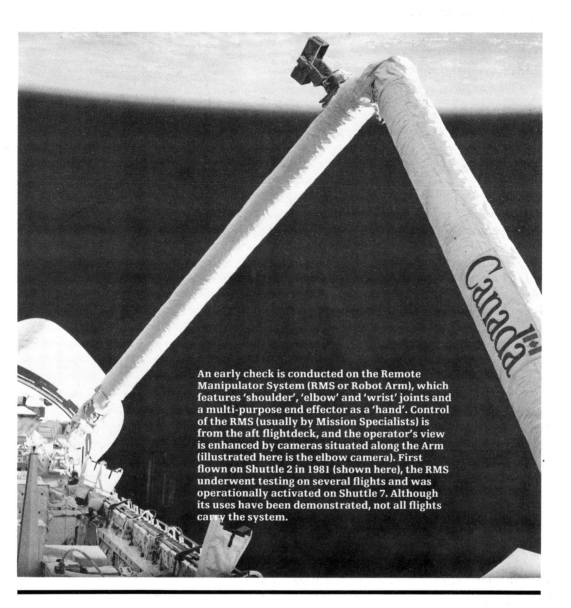

An early check is conducted on the Remote Manipulator System (RMS or Robot Arm), which features 'shoulder', 'elbow' and 'wrist' joints and a multi-purpose end effector as a 'hand'. Control of the RMS (usually by Mission Specialists) is from the aft flightdeck, and the operator's view is enhanced by cameras situated along the Arm (illustrated here is the elbow camera). First flown on Shuttle 2 in 1981 (shown here), the RMS underwent testing on several flights and was operationally activated on Shuttle 7. Although its uses have been demonstrated, not all flights carry the system.

special programmes for the specific objectives of the mission are carried with alternates usually available as contingency safeguards.

Despite the hard-working computers the ground teams at Houston still monitor every part of a flight including the functions which could, if necessary, be left to automatic systems. This vigilance is vital, although the room full of Flight Controllers familiar from the days of the Moonshots has been replaced by much smaller groups of specialists. The aim of the Space Transportation System is to reduce the number of ground controllers to just four. In practice there are always more specialists involved in following the progress

of a flight, but the intention to reduce the expensive manpower has been pursued aggressively.

The Capcom (Capsule Communicator, a term left over from the Mercury days) retains his role as spokesman for Mission Control and he has a key part to play in the maintenance of flightcrew morale. Traditionally the Capcom is an astronaut and, as link-man between the two basic archetypes of space operations (the pilot and the scientist), his function is diplomatic as much as communicative. There have been occasional disagreements between flightcrew and Mission Control and this is when the Capcom really earns his salary.

MAIN FLIGHTDECK CONTROL PANEL LAYOUT

1 Lighting panel, Star Tracker controls, general purpose computer controls.

2 TACAN controls, aft left and right RCS controls.

3 Radar altimeter instruments and lighting controls, OMS and forward RCS controls.

4 GPC status panel, cabin pressure and atmosphere displays.

5 Cryo system and fuel cell displays. 6RCS/OMS pressure and propellant quantity displays, mission elapsed time display.

7 Cabin windows.

8 Panel in front of Commander includes air data, acceleration rate, attitude and altitude displays, landing gear and RCS controls and Abort Mode controls.

9 Three CRT displays present flight parameters.

10 Panel in front of Pilot includes hydraulics and APU displays as well as duplicating Commander's primary flight instruments.

11 Cabin atmosphere, fire-suppression, body flap, attitude and nosewheel steering controls are to left of Commander.

12 Control column.

13 & 14 DAP input is between Commander and Pilot; central console includes OMS, FCS, SSME, body flap and attitude controls, Orbital DAP panel, ET ans SRB separation instruments, air data probe controls, DFI recorders, payload safing and emergency lighting switches.

15 Rudder pedals in front of both seats.

16 To right of Pilot, panels include propellant dump switches, APU controls, ET umbilical door controls and power distribution instrumentation.

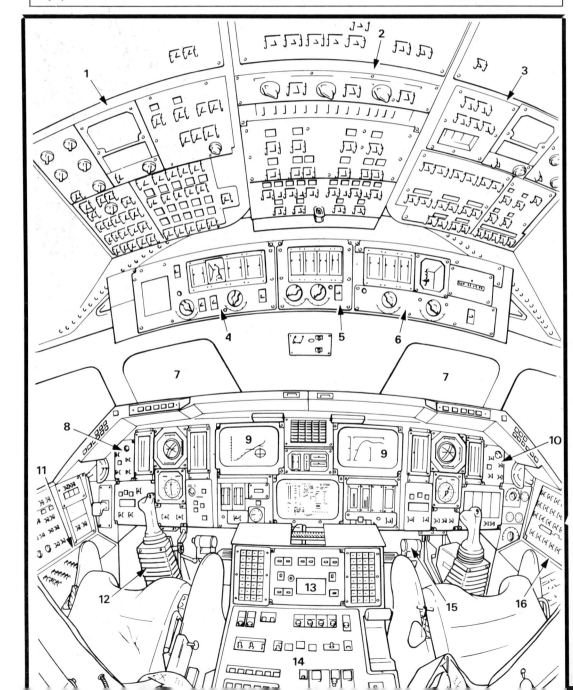

Above:
The vehicle in Earth orbit seen by an EVA crew-member flying the MMU during Shuttle 10. Sun shields cover the now vacant satellite cradles and the RMS is deployed from the payload bay.

One of the least likely aspects of ground monitoring ever to be automated is the medical supervision of the astronaut crew. Although Shuttle crews often include medical doctors it is the Flight Surgeon on the ground who decides what action is to be taken in the event of health problems in space. With flights lasting a week or more these can range from colds to dehydration due to space sickness. Serious orthopaedic injuries in the zero-G environment have so far been unknown but each Shuttle carries a medical kit equipped to deal with emergencies not only in space but also in the event of a crash landing in a remote area.

Daily private medical interviews with each crew member are conducted during a flight and many minor adjustments to schedules have resulted.

On this flight, so far the Commander has no worries about the health of his crew. They are all full of enthusiasm and no one as yet has experienced any nausea (or SAS). This is encouraging because as well as the satellite launches there is a complicated spacewalk on the flight plan.

Among the tasks routinely carried out by the Shuttle are:

Satellite launch, retrieval, refuelling.
Satellite repair.
Earth observations.
Optical and radar ground mapping.
Medical experiments.
Orbital laboratory experiments.
Astronomical observations.

The first major objective on this mission is to launch two communications satellites on behalf of a Third World country. The large investment is part of a growing nation's modernisation programme, so the crew will be expected to live up to the motto of the Space Transportation System: 'We deliver.'

Moving to the Aft Crew Station, the Commander prepares to prove the point.

SATELLITE OPERATIONS

Mission Control 'Houston is with you through Hawaii for eight minutes.'
Commander 'Roger. We have started to manoeuvre to deploy attitude.'
Mission Control 'We see that.'

During this last hour of the Pre-Deploy Procedure there is a heavy workload; from now on every aspect of the satellite's performance will be monitored for signs of trouble. Powering up of its internal systems has already begun.

This kind of operation is the bread and butter of the Space Transportation System. To be commercially viable it must be able to place satellites in orbit, especially geosynchronous ('Geo') orbit where communication satellites operate. As the Shuttle can go no higher than 690 miles (1,110km) — and even that would be exceptional — it can only take such a payload part of the way. The rest of the trip must be accomplished by a rocket attached to the satellite. NASA has four such rockets.

The smallest is the Payload Assist Module D, or 'PAM D'. This is used for light payloads which would earlier have been launched by the Delta disposable rocket (hence the 'D'). For larger loads previously entrusted to the Atlas rocket there is PAM A. Much larger loads use the Inertial Upper Stage (IUS).

Left:
Layout of aft crew station.

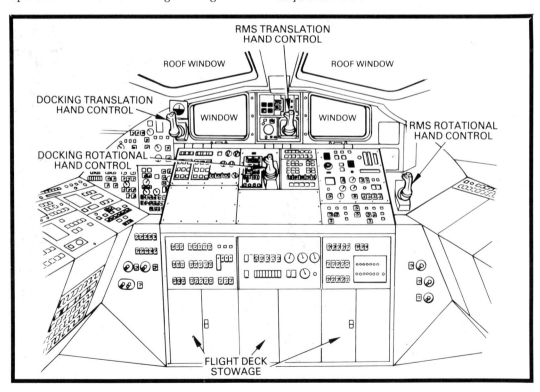

The fourth rocket is the Centaur Upper Stage, produced by General Dynamics. This immensely powerful unit is needed for very long-range space probes such as the Jupiter missions. It is somewhat controversial because it is a combination of liquid oxygen and liquid hydrogen: carrying Centaur would place these volatile substances in the Shuttle's payload bay for the first time. Originally it was planned that only *Challenger* and *Atlantis* would carry the Centaur. After the *Challenger* disaster, however, *Discovery* was modified to accept the unit.

The appropriate rocket unit is attached to the payload before it is taken into orbit in the Shuttle's cargo bay. Once in space the satellite is released and after adequate separation from the Orbiter has been achieved the rocket is fired to place it in Geo orbit. In the case of a PAM launch the craft is spun on a turntable before springs push it out of the bay. The

spinning counteracts any lopsidedness in the thrust from the PAM's nozzle which could result from the uneven burning to which small solid propellant rockets are prone.

The much larger IUS is more unwieldy and is attached to the payload bay sill. Once in space it is 'craned' over the side by the RMS Arm. In all cases a sufficient time is allowed for the satellite to distance itself from the Shuttle before firing; at least 45 minutes are needed, or the ignition could endanger the Orbiter. TV cameras on the Arm are used to observe the eventual firings.

If the astronaut crew is unable to provide visual confirmation of the firing, the ground teams will not know if the deployment was successful until telemetry is received from the satellite in Geo orbit. This can take several tense hours and when the signals are finally received there is a cheer of relief. If the deployment has failed the planning of a possible rescue mission to retrieve or repair the satellite starts immediately.

Because of limited room in the payload bay a satellite has to be carried into orbit in a 'stowed' position, usually with its vertical axis parallel to the Shuttle's fore-and-aft axis (this also protects the satellite from the acceleration stresses of the launch). Before deployment, therefore, the payload must be raised at

Below:
Mission Commander Bob Crippen at the primary Shuttle satellite deployment station on aft flightdeck of *Challenger* during the seventh Shuttle mission (1983).

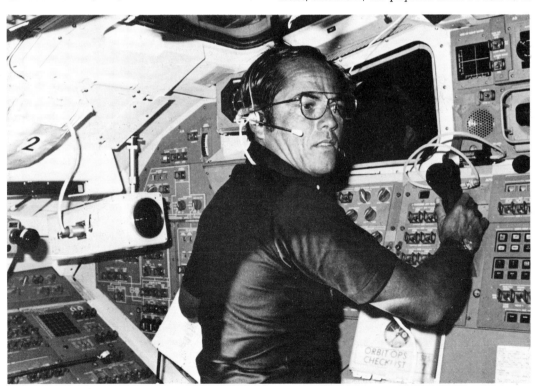

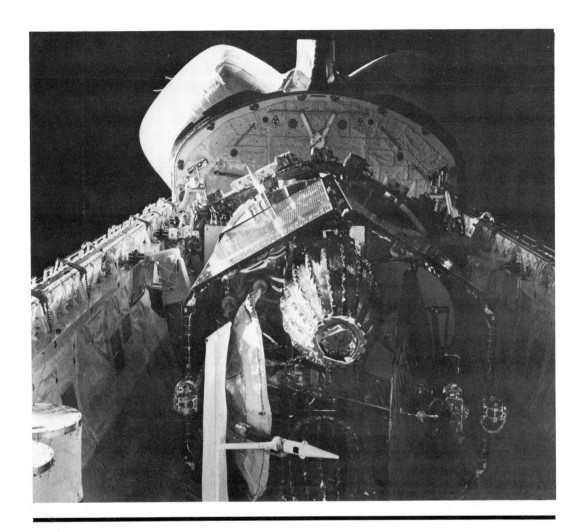

an angle to the bay. A tilt table is used, which must be lowered again after deployment, otherwise closure of the payload bay doors will be inhibited. If the lowering mechanism fails, a spacewalking astronaut will enter the bay to lower the table manually, for the Shuttle can not return to earth with the doors open. This operation was successfully demonstrated in simulation on the very first Shuttle spacewalk.

Not all satellites need to be in Geo orbit. Those which can function in Low Earth Orbit (Leo) can be deployed by the RMS Arm. If necessary these loads may occupy most of the cargo bay; it is thus possible to launch very large payloads such as the Long Duration Exposure Facility (LDEF) at only a fraction of the cost of a disposable rocket flight.

The LDEF (pronounced Eldeff) is designed to carry experiments which simply need a prolonged exposure to space, say a year at a time. Essentially it is a cylindrical rack on to which a number of experiment packages are attached — it is an orbital Christmas tree. It represents the effort being made at NASA to develop multi-function systems which can be adapted to the needs of different customers, the standardisation approach to the Space Transportation System.

Payloads like the LDEF which are designed to be returned eventually to Earth demonstrate not only the unique flexibility of the Shuttle concept but also the fundamental importance of the RMS Arm and, of course, the Mission Specialists who operate it.

Another standardisation concept of great potential is the Multi-Mission Modular Space-craft (MMS). This is simply a set of kit units which can be assembled to form the basic components of a satellite with the necessary

Left:

The primary operation for most Shuttle flights is the deployment of commercial and scientific satellites, usually accomplished early in the mission. This view shows a stowed Tracking & Data Relay Satellite A (TDRS/A) with an Inertial Upper Stage (IUS) in the payload bay of *Challenger* during Shuttle 6 (1983).

Below:

RMS control panel.

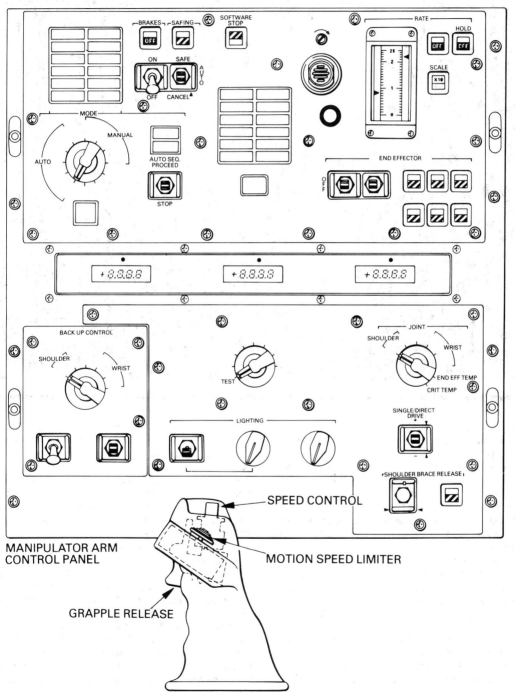

MANIPULATOR ARM
CONTROL PANEL

SPEED CONTROL

MOTION SPEED LIMITER

GRAPPLE RELEASE

control systems, communications antennae and experiment packages all in standardised form. The beauty of this idea is not only that it greatly reduces the cost of satellite construction but that standard parts which fail can be replaced with spares 'off the shelf'.

Backbone of the MMS is a mounting frame or Truss on to which the experiment package is secured. On to the other side of the Truss are attached the Power System Module, the Communications & Data Handling Module, the Attitude Control System Module and the solar panels which catch sunlight for conversion into electrical energy. A standard High Gain Antenna relays telemetry to Earth.

Although the first MMS spacecraft, the Solar Maximum mission, was launched by Delta rocket, the system is specifically designed for use with the Shuttle and all the necessary grapples and hand-holds are provided, the absence of which can greatly complicate any rescue mission.

In the event, Solar Max went unserviceable after a set of fuses blew out in orbit, and the prime task of Shuttle 11 was to repair the damage. As the whole concept of the MMS is ease of construction and repair this objective was an important one in terms of the creditability of the STS.

After notching up a first with the deployment of an LDEF, the Shuttle 11 astronauts proceeded with the attempted repair of Solar Max. Primarily their job was to replace the defunct Attitude Control Module with a new one. The first attempt was not successful: astronauts Nelson and Van Hoften 'went EVA' and Nelson, flying a Manned Manoeuvering unit (MMU), attempted to dock with the tumbling satellite. After a docking equipment failure he courageously tried to steady Solar Max manually. This proved far more difficult than expected and the alternative plan, to grab the craft with the RMS Arm, was put into operation. This too presented difficulties, and a team at NASA's Goddard Centre sweated through the night as the astronauts made repeated attempts to grapple Solar Max.

The efforts in space included work during the night-time passes (which occured every 90 minutes) during which the ailing MMS was floodlit by lights mounted on the RMS Arm. Eventually, after a second EVA which broke the STS spacewalk endurance record, the satellite was brought under control and the repair was successfully completed. The MMS concept had been proved, albeit with some hard work.

This mission provided perhaps the ultimate proof of the flexibility of the RMS Arm as well, for the device was used in a number of different modes and was called to the rescue when the efforts of spacewalkers failed. It was used to grapple the satellite and also as a vantage point from which floodlights and TV cameras could be trained on the work area. Later it provided stability for the EVA astronauts as they carried out difficult tasks in the vacuum of space. This is part of the Arm's design function, a work platform being available for attachment to the Arm's End Effector (or hand) on which an astronaut can ride. Relieved of the need to be forever steadying himself in the weightless environment, he can reserve his efforts for the operational task.

Even when Solar Max had been retrieved the Arm was still vital, as it was used to anchor the satellite while tests were carried out to verify that the repair had been successful.

Operated by its Mission Specialist controller, the Arm is the basic 'spade' of work in space, and despite its deceptively simple-looking controls it requires great skill to handle. The same natural aptitudes are needed as in flying an aircraft, especially the mental ability to orientate one's movements within a changing set of references. The Mission Specialist watches the Arm through the windows of the Aft Crew Station (in the rear bulkhead and also in the cabin roof). He (or she) must control the Arm in three dimensions with these two basic fields of vision, one horizontal, the other vertical. During this time the Orbiter itself is probably manoeuvring about three axes, and the target satellite may also be tumbling or changing position relative to the Shuttle. It is therefore quite easy for the operator to become disoriented, especially as a continuous commentary describing the movements of the RMS will be needed to reduce the danger of it colliding with hardware or EVA astronauts. RMS training is therefore rigorous, and the Mission Specialist who operates the Arm is perhaps the unsung hero of the STS, the glamour being attached to spacewalkers and flightcrew.

The process of grappling nearby targets with the RMS, potentially a hazardous one, is called Proximity Operations or Prox Ops. The Shuttle Pilot and Commander work alongside the Mission Specialist during Prox Ops because the manoeuvring of the Orbiter itself is as crucial as the accurate use of the Arm. If, for example, an EVA astronaut were cast adrift by some mishap the Shuttle would have to manoeuvre rapidly to rescue him. This was

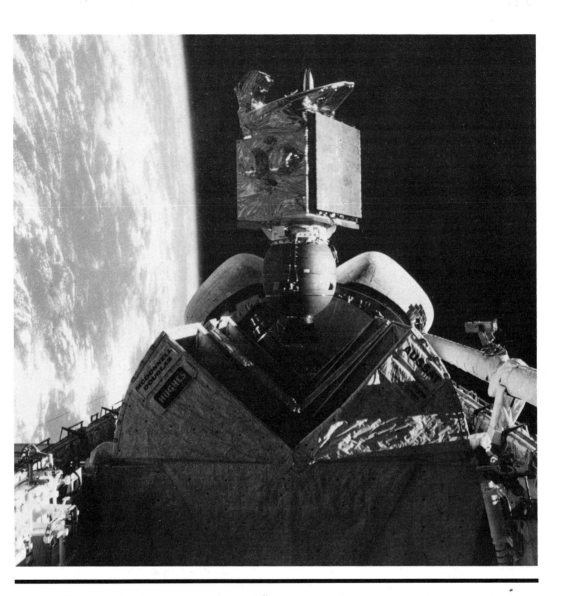

simulated on Shuttle 10 when a foot restraint broke loose from the cargo bay. Bruce McCandless was spacewalking along the bay when this happened and Commander Vance Brand quickly guided the Shuttle after the erring component. McCandless worked his way to the OMS pods and was able to reach up and grab the foot restraint. Had this object been an astronaut in distress, his life would have been saved.

Prox Ops are thus a team effort, the Commander and Mission Specialist side by side at the controls in the Aft Crew Station while spacewalkers and ground personnel play their own part in the accomplishment of the mission objectives.

Above:

The most common type of Shuttle satellite deployment involves a McDonnell-Douglas Payload Assist Module (PAM) upper stage, the sphere beneath the satellite shown here. An Australian AUSSAT spacecraft is seen rising from the payload bay of *Discovery* during Shuttle 20 (1985) while the crew monitors it with RMS cameras.

Stowed for launch in special cradles, the satellite PAM-D is spun to 52rpm before spring-ejection away from Shuttle prior to the ignition of the PAM-D motor which boosts it to operational altitude. A Shuttle is capable of either four PAM-D deployments, three PAM-D2 deployments, two 'frisbee' deployments or one IUS or Centaur deployment per flight.

33

In a thorough workout of Prox Ops on Shuttle 7 the German satellite SPAS was placed in orbit by the RMS Arm. The Shuttle was then manoeuvred in formation with it, while crew members took it in turns to guide the Arm and the Orbiter. The Arm proved very successful in a series of tests with the SPAS, being manoeuvred into the vicinity of the satellite in 'coarse' mode, then being switched to 'vernier' mode for the more precise movements necessary to contact and manipulate the payload. In another test on the same mission the Shuttle's thrusters were fired directly at the SPAS to see what effect this had. The blasts tumbled the satellite but caused no damage. Commander Bob Crippen commented: 'It's a credit to the engineers who put the SPAS together that it could take the kind of hits that it took.' This rough handling was all part of the test objectives of SPAS: other payloads would not have received such callous treatment!

Now, once again the Shuttle is about to launch a satellite. The digital autopilot has placed the Orbiter in the deployment attitude. Spin-up of the payload is under way, the Spin Table reaching 50rpm. The satellite is now operating on its own internal power. There are 10 minutes left.

Above:
The Long Duration Exposure Facility (LDEF) was designed for the STS. Containing experiment racks and without a propulsion system, LDEF enables a variety of small experiments to be carried on one vehicle. Deployed from Shuttle 11 in 1984 it was to be retrieved and returned to Earth in 1985 for refurbishment and reuse, but several delays to the programme caused this to be postponed.

Mission Control 'Looking good for deploy.'
The Shuttle is now approaching a communications switch-over point.

Mission Control 'Thirty seconds to loss of signal Hawaii; TDRS next in three minutes.'
The automatic sequencer which will cause the satellite to be spring-ejected from the payload bay is armed. Everything is ready. Houston is now in contact again, the TDRS satellite beaming the transmissions across space.

Commander 'We have motion; the satellite is going clear of the bay. Clear of the tail now. That was a good deploy!'
Beside him one of the Mission Specialists adds:
'It's going, guys, and we're taking pictures!'

Mission Control 'Roger, we copy a good deploy on time.'

Commander 'Good sunshield closing too. The PAM looks beautiful out there. No weather problems up here! We're deploying the RMS (camera) now to monitor the burn.'

Mission Control Roger; we expect an 86-second time on that burn,'

As the Shuttle moves to the 'Window Protect' attitude, facing away from the coming rocket ignition, the satellite is no longer visible to the naked eye, but a camera on the RMS Arm enables monitoring to continue. Still moving with the energy imparted by the deployment spring, the PAM and its cargo head steadily away from the Orbiter. As more than half an hour passes the separation increases towards the safe margin. Finally . . .

Commander 'We see the burn!'
As the PAM ignites the spinning satellite accelerates towards its new home 22,300 miles (35,887km) above the Earth. The crew watch the burn, counting the seconds.

Commander 'It faded after about 86 seconds; it was very impressive because all through the burn we could see lightning flashes all over the Earth.'

In the atmosphere below, the heavy rain which so nearly delayed the launch has turned into a violent thunderstorm. Already weather forecasters are trying to anticipate any resulting difficulty in the re-entry and landing phase, but to the crew in space all that is still far away.

AT HOME IN SPACE

Having been in space before, the Commander is not surprised by the sensations of weightlessness, but he still feels a kind of elation which is hard to describe. John Young, a veteran astronaut not given to overstatement, once called zero-G 'delightful'. As yet nobody has claimed to have found it unpleasant.

Perhaps the most surprising thing about it is the speed at which the human body adapts to the new environment. In space an astronaut can let go of an object without it falling to the ground. He can throw back the folds of his sleep-restraint and float out of bed. After his first flight the Commander found that it was re-adapting to Earth conditions which was the problem. Once, soon after landing, he absentmindedly let go of a coffee cup and was surprised when it fell and shattered.

There is really no comparison between living conditions on the Shuttle and those in the Mercury, Gemini and Apollo series of spacecraft. Skylab, the orbital workshop, gave US astronauts their first experience of long term exposure to zero-G in a reasonable working space and the benefits were to some extent offset by an increase in space-sickness. This suggested that the nausea might be partly the result of the unrestricted movement in three

Below:
The effect of the micro-gravity environment of Earth orbit upon teleprinter messages from Ground Control is evident as Shuttle 16 Commander Bobko attempts to gather reams of paper in the mid deck of *Discovery*.

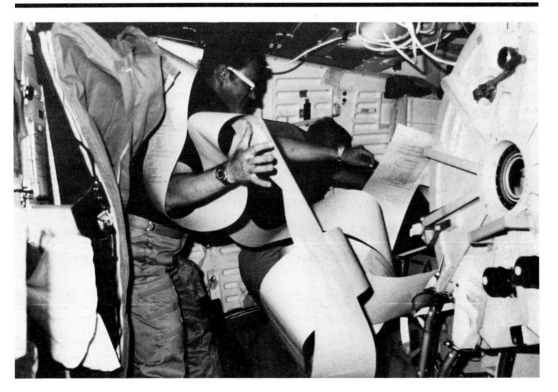

Left:
Shuttle 5 Commander Brand shaves with a safety razor and foam during his week-long mission. A towel floats by his legs, and attached to his calves are a checklist and radio communications pack. Astronauts may use a battery razor if they prefer.

Above:
Regular changing of lithium hydroxide canisters by the crew is part of the 'housekeeping' on every flight: astronaut Lousma is seen on mid deck of *Columbia* during its third mission. These canisters purify air for recycling to the cabin atmosphere.

dimensions. One interesting discovery was that there is no relationship between susceptibility to air sickness and cases of space sickness.

Having already deployed a satellite the astronauts have worked up an appetite. One of the Payload Specialists is now at the galley on the mid deck preparing a hot meal. This is another area in which there have been improvements since the early days. Food is still provided in the dehydrated and packaged form first developed for the Mercury flights,

although choice has widened. This type of fare has been a great success, despite its unappetising appearance, especially from an engineering point of view where the chief concern has been to prevent food particles from infiltrating the operational equipment. NASA was not amused when, in 1965, John Young took a corned beef sandwich into space, although at the same time the Russians were providing cakes for their crews!

At the Shuttle galley crew members share a cooking rota. As flights last only about a week a refrigerator (available on Skylab) is not thought necessary. Meals are served on airline-style trays and as well as the usual re-hydratable items the menu includes some things in their normal state, such as meat, bread, nuts, fruit, biscuits and candy bars. NASA has become less obsessed with the danger of crumbs, especially as powerful fans continually draw such free-floating objects to collection points where they can be dealt with using a vacuum cleaner.

Food tastes different in space, due to subtle physiological changes in the body and also because of the specialised preparation which it must undergo. On Shuttle 19/Spacelab 2, cans of Coke and Pepsi were evaluated. Astronauts found the drinks palatable, but the carbonation level was said to be too high.

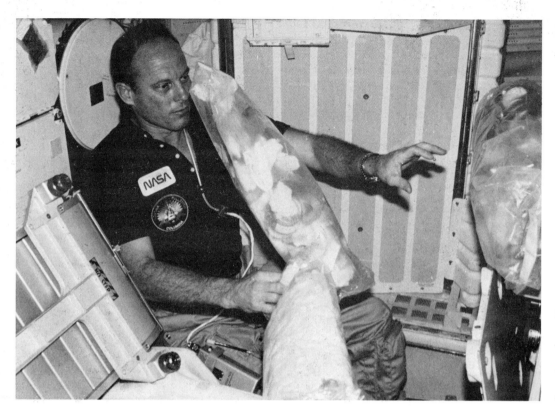

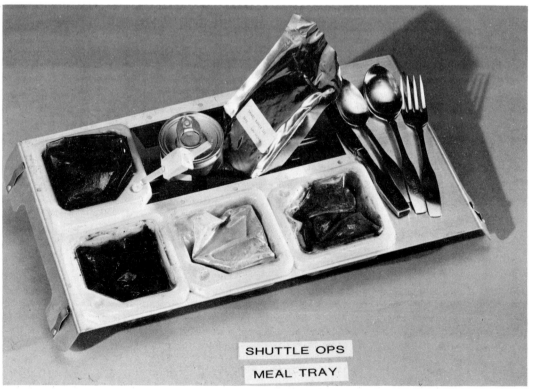

SHUTTLE OPS
MEAL TRAY

Waste disposal in orbit is achieved by stuffing rubbish into sealable plastic bags which are then jammed into lockers. Excess water is often dumped into space; this provided a media event in 1984 when the Shuttle 12 crew used the RMS to dislodge an icicle which blocked an overflow pipe, earning them the title 'Ice Busters'.

Left:
In pre-Shuttle days space meals were served in 'toothpaste' tubes or mushed in plastic bags. Shuttle cuisine includes hot meals from mid deck galley: the trays latch into recesses on the cabin walls, and crews can use ordinary knives and forks.

Above:
This floating globe of orange juice demonstrates how liquids react in weightlessness, delighting Joe Allen during Shuttle 5 (1982).

Hot food is not new in space but the use of a galley instead of self-heating packages improves efficiency and reduces the necessary storage area. All food is either cooked on board or heated or irradiated before the flight to eliminate bacteria. Each astronaut's daily diet is devised before the flight and its nutritional value calculated for sustained energy. A crew member's average daily intake is 3,000 dietary calories, the same as for an active person on Earth. In general the whole crew eats the same menu but allowances are made for individual preference.

Waste management, particularly that of human waste, still presents a problem. Earth gravity has a useful knack of tidying things up by drawing them to a focal point. In space it is not so, and a very small amount of uncontrolled waste can contaminate a large area. On Shuttle 17/Spacelab 3, which carried laboratory monkeys, cages proved inadequate to contain animal feed and droppings which then floated around the cabin. Commander Overmyer commented: 'Faeces in the cockpit is not much fun' and added ruefully: 'How many years did we tell them these cages would not work?' He sounded angry and he was; this sort of thing can ruin an astronaut's whole day.

The human toilet facilities are a little better. The lavatory consists of a commode on which the astronaut sits to perform normal bowel evacuation. It is essential that a tight seal is maintained between the buttocks and the seat, and the lapstrap originally used proved insufficient. Cushioned thigh bars are therefore swung across the seated astronaut's legs

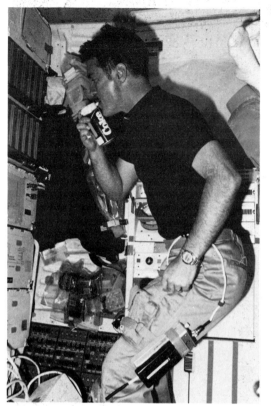

Above:

Later crews sampled a variety of refreshments. Fizzy drinks require special oral receptacles to retain a sparkle.

A urine collection device is available to males while the less conveniently designed female uses special sealed knickers. Super-absorbent fibres impregnated with a powerful disinfectant maintain reasonable safety from germs.

A luxury available on Skylab but not the Shuttle was a shower-bath, although there is a hand-washing facility with hot water. The Skylab shower was difficult to use and on the shorter duration of a Shuttle mission it is sufficient to rely on Personal Hygiene Kits. These include such items as deodorant, wet-wipes, hair-brushes and shaving kit.

Sleeping in weightlessness is not as simple as might be imagined. Although the absence of gravity makes a bed as such unnecessary, it is still required that some form of restraint be provided to prevent a sleeping astronaut from drifting about. Not only might the sleeper be disturbed by collisions with solid objects, but there is also a tendency in weightlessness for the arms to float up until the hands touch the face and cause a startled awakening.

A sleeping-bag-like restraint provides a degree of physical comfort and safety. As sleep follows a shift rota, masks and earmuffs are used to prevent disturbance by the working shift.

The Sleep Station is on the mid deck and comprises four bunks, three of which are horizontal to the deck. The other is vertical. In zero-G it does not matter which way 'up' one sleeps, and of course it is possible to lie on the floor, wall or ceiling of one's bunk compartment. Astronauts take it in turns to sleep but it is not necessary, for safety, to mount a 24-hour watch. Indeed it is considered better for crew-members to sleep simultaneously, although the size of a crew or the scheduling of tasks may preclude this.

By wearing a lightweight headset an astronaut can remain on-call while he rests. If it is necessary to wake him Mission Control can play an alarm signal.

The carriage for the first time of female astronauts in the US Space Programme has made preferable some degree of privacy which was impossible in smaller craft. The Shuttle incorporates a range of screens, cubicles and

and exert a gentle downward pressure. The waste material, assisted by suction, passes into a spinning drum called a 'slinger' which uses centrifugal force to deposit the faeces in a thin layer around its sides. Later the drum is exposed to the vacuum of space and this instantly freezes and dries the material, rendering it inert.

Urine collection is complicated slightly by the need to provide unisex equipment. A funnel-like device attached to a hose is situated at the front of the commode and can be used individually or together with the commode. It is not necessary to be seated to use this part of the equipment, but females must make sure that positive body contact is maintained with the funnel during use. Urine is collected in a tank and eventually dumped overboard.

Waste management when wearing an EVA pressure suit is rather more traditional. As in earlier days, the astronaut does it in his pants.

Facing page:
Attached to the huge External Tank (ET) and Solid Rocket Boosters (SRBs), *Discovery* leaves Launch Complex 39A at the start of its third mission (1985). Note the ice particles flaking away from the ET; also the circular entry hatch on the side of the vehicle, beneath its name, which gives access to the crew compartment.

Above:
STS-5 Commander Vance Brand (left) holds a
checklist while Pilot Overmyer points to data on
the CRT display. Note the cue sheets attached
around the console, and the effect of
weightlessness on flexible leads.

Below:
Anna Fisher emerges from a full sleep restraint
during Shuttle 14 in 1984. Married to a fellow
astronaut, Fisher was the first mother to fly in
space. Note the second sleep restraint above her.

Above right:
Zero G enhances the hairstyle of Judy Resnik as
she poses beside a sticker honouring a favourite
TV star: on most missions the crew decorate the
cabin with pictures and slogans to create a
homely environment. This picture was taken
during Resnik's first flight, Shuttle 12 (1984); her
next, tragically, ended in disaster.

hygiene needs but also the rather more demanding thirst of the Orbiter's cooling systems.

Once in space no special clothing is needed within the crew compartment. Each astronaut has a set of coveralls resembling a track suit, underwear, socks and lightweight shoes. Apart from the brassiere issued to females the attire is unisex. Most astronauts find a shirt and shorts combination the most comfortable. During the atmospheric part of the flight a helmet is worn, similar to that of a high-altitude pilot, while a G-suit covering the legs exerts a pressure which prevents blood from being driven away from the upper part of the body during positive-acceleration man-oeuvres.

Another item of spacewear is the cordless headset, a radio communication set which eliminates the need to plug into wall sockets. This is more convenient than the type first used which trailed wires around the cabin.

In the weightless environment there is no need to be seated while operating the Shuttle's controls and equipment. To float is as restful as to sit. Nor is there any difficulty in reaching the desired control; one can drift up to the ceiling or stand on one's head without effort. Although there is a ladder linking the two decks it is never used in space; astronauts just glide through the hatchway. Nevertheless there is a need for some kind of anchorage to hold a crewmember securely whenever he needs to exert a pressure or purchase on a control. If he tries to work unsecured he will be continually drifting about in reaction to the force he is exerting at his task. Foot restraints are therefore provided, the heights of which are fully adjustable.

Finally, despite all the hard work, there is always some time built into the schedule for relaxation and reflection. This is a serious psychological need. Spaceflight is a profound emotional experience and the long-duration flights of Skylab demonstrated that at least some scope for quiet contemplation is essential. As the Commander looks around his crew he notices how each one, whether old hand or rookie, is drawn periodically to the window. The view is spectacular, of course, but that is not the whole story; there is a need to look 'up' at the Earth, to savour the experience of being a part of the sky. 'It's kind of hard to keep my head in the cockpit here', he radioes to Mission Control. The Capcom at his console far below in Houston has not yet flown a mission, but he knows what the Commander means. They all do. 'We sure envy you guys', he acknowledges.

curtains, and personalised lockers are provided. A crew member has some freedom of choice as to the private items which may be carried. Personal Preference Kits (PPKs) may contain mascots, taped messages from well-wishers and other personal things. French Payload Specialist Patrick Baudry took some wine (not for on-orbit consumption!) to see if the taste was affected by space travel.

The improvements in comfort and privacy are a necessary part of normalising the space environment. Designs for future space stations even include soundproof sleeping rooms for couples who, in the jargon of NASA, are 'significantly relating'.

Perhaps the most basic requirement of all is breathable air. The Shuttle's air is chemically much closer to that of Earth than the atmosphere of earlier vehicles. An oxygen/nitrogen mix at 14.7lb/sq in (1,033g/sq cm) is used (the pressure can be varied if necessary) and the build-up of exhaled carbon dioxide is controlled by 'scrubbing' the air. Fans circulate the air through charcoal filters impregnated with lithium hydroxide and, apart from the periodic need to change a lithium hydroxide canister, the system runs itself.

The oxygen carried aboard has another important function; the Shuttle's electrical power is derived from three fuel cells in the equipment bay in the nose below the middeck. These cells combine oxygen and hydrogen to produce electricity and — an added bonus — water which is stored in two large tanks. These tanks supply not only the crew's drinking and

Years of preparation and planning go into each mission, which result in the Shuttle leaving the pad at T minus zero. This is *Challenger* in the early stages of construction at Rockwell's Palmdale plant in California before delivery to Kennedy Spaceflight Center in 1982. Clearly visible in this photo are the crew compartment module sitting in the lower fuselage shell, thermal blankets and support stringers.

Above:
An overall view of the forward flightdeck aboard the *Discovery* under construction by Rockwell International. Most of the display and control consoles are in place; the Commander's station is on the left and the pilot's is on the right.

Below:
This is one of the last photographs taken of *Columbia* before it was moved from the Palmdale, California manufacturing facility to Kennedy Space Center, Florida.

EXTRA-VEHICULAR ACTIVITY

After a sleep period the second satellite launch takes place, and Day 2 of the mission continues with onboard scientific experiments. Already, however, the Commander is preparing for the next major objective, an EVA scheduled for Day 3. As a flightdeck astronaut the Commander does not perform spacewalks, although he has been fully trained in this area. EVA is nowadays the preserve of the Mission Specialist.

There are three types of Shuttle EVA:

PLANNED When the mission includes such EVA tasks as satellite retrieval, repair and reufelling, or (as will become increasingly common) space construction work.

UNSCHEDULED When an unforeseen event calls for a spacewalk: the first example occurred on Shuttle 16 when a satellite failed after deployment and an EVA attempted to repair it.

CONTINGENCY When an emergency occurs (NASA prefers the word contingency). In the event of a Shuttle having to be abandoned the crew could be transferred to a rescue ship. As only two EVA suits are carried the unsuited crewmembers would have to travel in zip-up pressure balls called Personal Rescue Spheres.

All astronauts are given basic training in the principles of EVA and also in the use of the Sphere. Even in today's shirt-sleeves-in-space

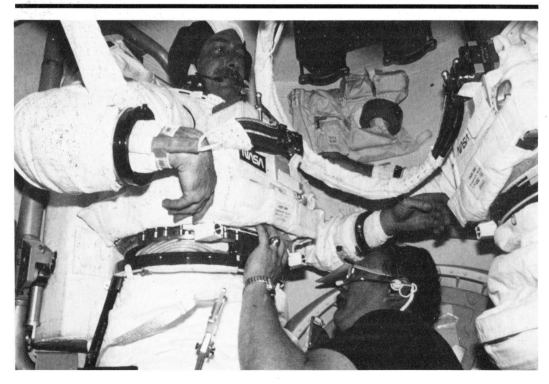

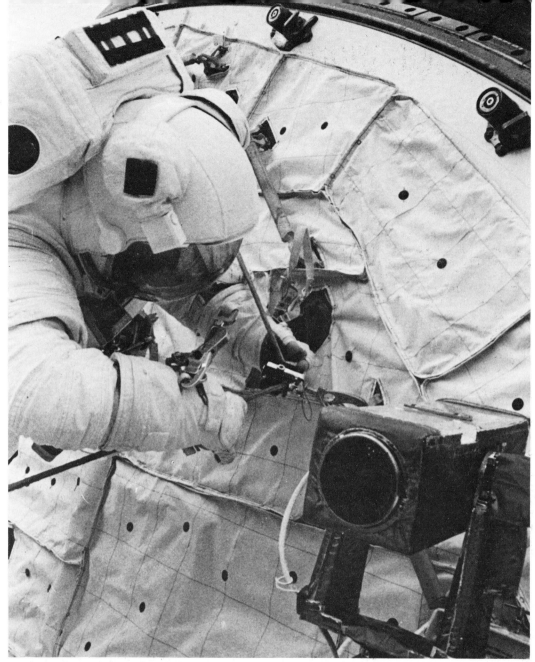

Left:
**Mission Specialists Hoffman and Griggs (just
visible right) prepare for the Shuttle 16 EVA,
with Commander Bobko assisting Hoffman to
join the Hard Upper Torso to the legs of his suit.
Located in the mid deck airlock of *Discovery*, the
suits are secured by foot restraints and
connected to the Orbiter's air supply until just
prior to EVA. Thumb rings help the wearer
retain the sleeves of the cooling garment and
communications are maintained via the 'Snoopy
hat' to the EVA partner, the rest of the crew and
Ground Control.**

Above:
**A Shuttle 6 EVA astronaut at the aft end of
Challenger. The picture shows a slide wire/
tether system, helmet lights, a payload bay TV
camera and the pulley wheels of the contingency
door-closing mechanism. Note the thermal
blanket insulation.**

Above:
In February 1981 NASA conducted a test firing of *Columbia's* main engines. Hold-down bolts secured the vehicle to the mobile launch platform during this formal rehearsal for the April 1981 first mission.

Right:
Emerging from clouds of exhaust flame, *Challenger* clears the tower. The lightning deflector atop the structure is visible to the left of the Orbiter.

Top right:
This view from beneath *Challenger* illustrates the contrast of the smoke efflux from the Solid Rocket Boosters with the almost smokeless liquid rocket exhausts from the Space Shuttle main engines.

48

era a spacesuit is a cumbersome item requiring special training.

On this mission the EVA task is a repair. A Mission Specialist will exit the Orbiter, don a Manned Manoeuvering Unit and 'fly' across to a target satellite. There he will connect himself with it and attempt to guide it back to the payload bay. At the same time a second spacewalker will be on hand to assist if his companion runs into difficulties.

Day 3 of the flight begins with an atmosphere of mounting excitement, enhanced when Mission Control light-heartedly plays *The Daring Young Man on the Flying Trapeze* over the radio in honour of the impending spacewalk. Already the Shuttle has achieved an automatic rendezvous with the target satellite using special software fed into the digital autopilot. Now the satellite is visible from the flightdeck windows as it awaits its visitor.

Two hours before the scheduled time of the EVA the two space-walkers go to the mid deck to put on the inner layers of their suits. Over basic underwear a Cooling & Ventilation Garment is donned, together with the male's urine collection device. Then they float up through the hatch on to the flightdeck to put on their helmets for the tedious but vital pre-breathing. The purpose of this is to breathe pure oxygen (for at least two hours) and thus purge all the nitrogen from the body: to enter a pure-oxygen, reduced pressure environment such as a spacesuit without this

pre-breathing would cause the nitrogen to bubble out of the bloodstream inducing agony (known as the bends) in the joints.

Eventually, with about 45 minutes left before the EVA, the two Mission Specialists go to the mid deck and enter the airlock so as to continue the suiting-up. Over the cooling garment which circulates water around the body they pull the trouser or Lower Torso section of the two-piece suit. The suit is more correctly called an EVA Mobility Unit or EMU. It comes in a range of standard sizes and includes a drink-dispenser, worn inside the helmet.

The upper part of the EMU is known as the Hard Upper Torso or HUT; this has a built-in life support backpack. Even in weightlessness the HUT is unwieldy and has to be positioned carefully to enable the wearer to squirm up into it from a crouch. Nevertheless the EMU is much simpler than the moonwalking suit from which it was derived.

Loops attached to the arms of the cooling garment fit around the thumbs to prevent the sleeves riding up inside the HUT during EVA. Then the joining seal between the suit's upper and lower section is closed. A soft helmet or 'Snoopy hat' with radio earphones and microphones, a hard helmet with visor, and a pair of close-fitting gloves complete the outfit.

A panel on the chest of the EMU provides a digital readout of oxygen and pressure levels. It also has a malfunction warning system. The dials of this panel use back to front 'mirror

Facing page, top:
Slide wires assist mobility in the payload bay, as illustrated by Shuttle 14 Mission Specialist Gardner moving forward along the door hinge line (or longeron). Attached to the slide wire by a safety tether, the astronaut uses handrails which run the length of the payload bay.

Above:
Foot restraints can be attached directly to the payload bay. Note the open EVA hatch in this view, taken by an astronaut riding the RMS.

Left:
'Pinky' Nelson and 'Ox' Van Hoften (left, on a portable foot restraint) work on 'Solar Max', replacing an electrics box and associated wiring. After successful repair 'Solar Max' was redeployed into orbit by the RMS to resume its full scientific programme.

Far left:

In August 1985 Shuttle 20 approached the Leasat satellite in order to repair a faulty electrical circuit which had prevented its activation during Shuttle 16. Once the satellite had been slowed manually by astronaut van Hoften, who had been attached to the RMS platform, astronaut Bill Fisher worked at the side of the satellite to attach an electrical bypass system. Subsequently ground controllers activated the satellite several weeks after the astronauts had returned to Earth.

Left:

The world's first human satellite! Astronaut Bruce McCandless performed a long range, untethered EVA during Shuttle 10 in 1984, venturing 300ft away from *Challenger*.

Below:

For complex scientific experiments the Shuttle can carry a Space Laboratory in its payload bay. Simply called Space Lab it can be used in a variety of configurations with or without manned modules.

writing' to enable the astronaut to read them from a polished reflector plate mounted on the cuff. Bright sunlight has been found to impair legibility in these displays but in general they have worked well.

With the two Mission Specialists in the airlock, head-to-toe in a '69' position, the Commander informs Houston of progress.

Commander 'Roger, Houston, we've got the hatch closed and we're waiting for a Go for depress on time.'
Mission Control 'Affirmative; you have a Go for depress.'

Inside the airlock the suits have been tested for leaks with their internal pressure at maximum. No leaks have been found and the suits are returned to the normal pressure. Now the airlock atmosphere can be vented and the hatch opened to allow the spacewalkers to pass through into the cargo bay.

Commander 'Airlock depress valve to zero.'

The airlock itself is a movable unit, cylindrical in shape, which can occupy a number of positions inside the Orbiter. The usual location is inside the crew compartment on the mid deck, but the hatch in the bulkhead of the Orbiter is designed so that the airlock can be attached to either side of it. It is therefore possible to mount the airlock on the outside of the bulkhead, in the cargo bay. The deciding factor is whether the particular needs of the mission place a premium on workspace in the crew compartment or the cargo bay. In the case of a Spacelab mission the Spacelab entry tunnel can be fitted directly on to the bulkhead so that the airlock can be positioned against the tunnel rather than the bulkhead.

On all Shuttle EVAs one of the spacewalkers is in charge of the operation while his companion acts as a backup. The leader is designated EV1 and wears red bands round his arms and legs for identification.

Commander 'Roger, Houston, the hatch is open; EV1 is half way out. They're configuring the airlock, getting ready for EV2 to come out.'

Whereas spacewalkers of earlier generations always remained tethered to their vehicles by an umbilical cord, Shuttle astronauts have self-contained life support systems in their suits. This new freedom is essential when using the Manned Manoeuvering Unit. Once in space the astronaut can move around the cargo bay unrestricted by life-support or communication cords. There is, however, a range of wires to which he may attach himself to facilitate movement and to enable him to free both hands for work. The wires run the length of the bay along the fuselage longerons, and there is a pulley which can guide the spacewalker from one side of the ship to the other without requiring him to expend effort in changing his position. These devices were demonstrated on the very first Shuttle EVA.

To provide further support while the Astronaut performs EVA tasks, a platform is available on to which he can attach himself. This, together with the handrails, slidewires and pulleys, enables the spacewalker to work in the payload bay in reasonable safety, free of the risk of drifting away or colliding with hard surfaces. Many EVA tasks call for work well away from the payload bay. For this type of activity the Manned Manoeuvering Unit (MMU) has been developed. This device roughly resembles the back and arms of an armchair. On the back of the chair the fuel and control systems are carried and the astronaut flies this personal spacecraft using handgrips which are situated on the armrests. The MMU uses 24 reaction control thrusters and the procedures for manoeuvring are basically consistent with the operation of the Shuttle and the RMS Arm. This eases training and makes less likely any misunderstanding between crewmembers during an EVA.

To guard against the remote possibility of an MMU pilot becoming lost in space a radio transponder beacon is carried as well as a flashing light for visual reference. Communications are available in MMU-to-Orbiter and MMU-to-ground modes, and so the isolation of the free-flying spaceman which appears so stark on TV news pictures is not really as much of a separation as it might seem.

The two EVA Mission Specialists now pass in turn into the Orbiter's cargo bay. They have already connected themselves to the slide-wires; now as they pass through the outer door of the airlock the cavernous bay looms around them.

At the far end of the bay the two satellites have gone; they were launched on the first and second day of the mission and are now more than 22,000 miles above the orbit of the Shuttle. Despite their departure the payload bay still seems crowded to the two spacewalkers.

EV1 casts his eyes over the scene; it is a treasure house of scientific equipment, gleaming white in the unhindered sunlight. To the right is the uncradled RMS Arm, an important tool on this EVA. Below it under the sill of the bay a line of canisters house the 'Getaway

Left:
Following the failure of two satellites (deployed successfully by the Shuttle 10 mission) to achieve operational orbit, NASA organised a rescue on a later flight. Shuttle 14 was assigned the task of retrieving the satellites for return to Earth. The capture of both satellites was achieved in the same way. Approaching from beneath, the astronaut inserts the specially designed 'Stinger' capture device into the engine bell, then the tumbling satellite is steadied and returned to the Shuttle with the help of a second EVA crew member.

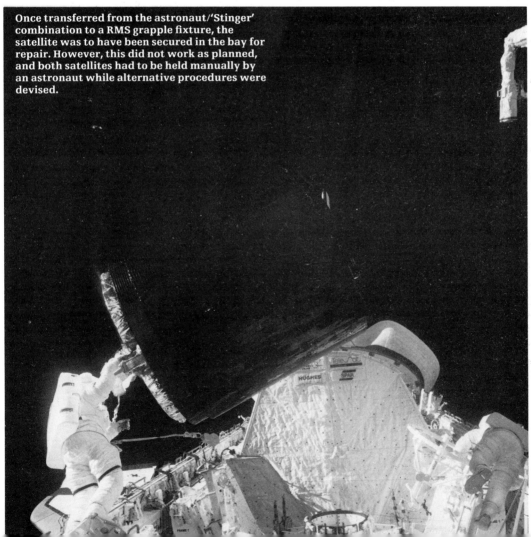

Once transferred from the astronaut/'Stinger' combination to a RMS grapple fixture, the satellite was to have been secured in the bay for repair. However, this did not work as planned, and both satellites had to be held manually by an astronaut while alternative procedures were devised.

Above:
Touchdown! *Columbia* lands at Edwards AFB on 8 December 1983. The effects of the spaceflight on the Shuttle's hull are readily apparent.

Inset top:
The crew emerge when vehicle safing is complete.

Specials', self-contained automatic experiments from universities and other customers. Across the centre of the bay more modular equipment waits for EV2 to perform his tasks.

EV1's MMU is attached to the outside of the cabin bulkhead to his right. He approaches the Unit, inspects it and then carefully backs himself into it. Helped by EV2, he locks the MMU on to the backpack of his suit and also attaches a special plate to the chest section. This plate is equipped with a docking device which he will use to connect himself to the target satellite. The MMU arm controllers are then swung out to the flight position and EV1 is ready to go.

Now free of the sliding tethers, EV1 gently pushes himself away from the bulkhead. As he floats upwards he fires the MMU thrusters; silent puffs of propellant nudge him away from the Shuttle.

Gradually he approaches the target satellite; as he draws nearer he clearly sees its slight spinning motion. Although slow, this spinning will have to be damped out before he can achieve a docking with the target.

It takes EV1 all of 15 minutes to cross the 200ft of space which separates the Orbiter from the satellite. The trip is timed so that he will arrive between the rotating solar panels which extend, winglike, from it. As he approaches he uses the MMU thrusters to match the satellite's rotation rate.

When at last he is within arm's reach he aims the docking probe, which protrudes from the T bar plate on his chest, into its attachment socket. He thrusts it home, but the click of a successful latching is not felt. He tries again; with no success.

EV1 'I'm having trouble with the T-Pad: I don't think I'm getting enough penetration there.'

He tries again, unaware that a small grommet which holds thermal insulation on the satellite is preventing the docking probe from achieving the necessary 3in of penetration.

EV1 'Something's inhibiting the Trunnion.'

The satellite is now beginning to react to the impacts as EV1 tries to force the docking probe into position. Already rotating, it now starts to pitch and yaw as well. With MMU fuel running low as the thrusters are repeatedly fired in an attempt to steady the satellite, the time is approaching for a tough decision.

Commander 'I think you should come back pretty soon. We'll try to grapple that fellow with the RMS.'

With the satellite now becoming unstable the use of the Arm will be difficult unless the target can be steadied. EV1 grabs hold of one of the solar wings and again uses the MMU thrusters to damp out the yawing motion. Eventually, after 35 minutes of free flight, he returns to the payload bay.

Meanwhile EV2 has been busy in the bay. Earlier in the mission an antenna failed to fold away automatically and EV2 has managed to stow it manually so that it will not inhibit the closure of the payload bay doors. He has also taken several photographs of EV1's efforts, to

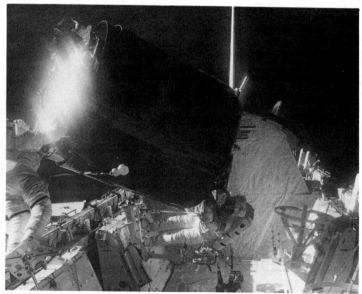

Left:
Astronaut Joe Allen held both satellites while Gardner attached them manually to the pallet in the payload bay of *Discovery*. These two successful demonstrations of man's usefulness in space were instrumental in the return of the satellites to Earth for later relaunch.

Above:

In what appears to have become the motto of Shuttle EVAs Shuttle 14 astronaut Gardner displays a 'For Sale' sign promoting the success of Shuttle satellite retrieval, repair and recovery operations.

add to the footage from the TV camera mounted on the RMS arm.

EV1 backs the MMU into its housing and disconnects himself from it. Then he secures himself to the slidewire system and joins EV2 as the Orbiter is manoeuvred to within 40ft of the satellite. Now the difficult job of grappling the target with the RMS is attempted.

After a worrying hour the attempts are successful. By this time the Shuttle is on the night-time side of the Earth with the payload bay illuminated by floodlights.

The grappled satellite is now guided into the bay by the RMS Arm and the two spacewalkers attach a retaining device to hold it securely to the bay sill. EV1 notices he has worn away a whole layer of insulation from his gloves and he carefully inspects the damage before continuing with the heavy manual work.

With the satellite anchored to the payload bay a work platform is attached to the RMS Arm. EV2 now mounts this platform, secures himself to a foot restraint, and the RMS operator carefully cranes him to the positions required for the repair of the satellite. EV2 replaces several defective instrument packages with new items.

At this stage in the flight plan there is plenty of flexibility: if the repair had not gone smoothly the spacewalkers would have been recalled inside the Orbiter for a rest period, and the remainder of their tasks would have been rescheduled for the following day. The replacement of the packages has not proved difficult, however, and the decision is made to complete the whole operation in the same EVA.

EV2 now dismounts the RMS and the two astronauts watch as the Arm is re-connected with the grapple on the satellite. When this is achieved the satellite is released from its cradle in the payload bay and the Arm gently shifts it away. Finally it is released. Now fully operational again, the satellite can be replaced in its correct orbit by remote signals from the ground.

The two Mission Specialists prepare to re-enter the airlock. In the Orbiter's Aft Crew Compartment the RMS controller calls to them:

'Take a bow for the elbow camera!'

The spacewalkers oblige, and the RMS-mounted TV camera records their relief that the EVA task has been accomplished successfully.

EV2 takes a last look at the spectacular scenery, the coast of Baja California emerging in the dawn above him. Then it is time for him to rejoin his crewmates on board the Shuttle.

SCIENCE IN SPACE

With the two EVA Mission Specialists safely back on board, the most spectacular part of the mission's revenue-earning work is complete. Nevertheless, the scene inside the Orbiter is still one of intense activity. Payload Specialists are busy conducting medical experiments and also taking photographs as part of a ground-mapping survey. In the crew compartment as well as the open pay-load bay, scientific instrument packages are collecting and recording data.

One of the most important functions of the Space Transportation System is this ability to transport the laboratory into space, where scientists can study not only space itself but also chemical and physical phenomena in the conditions of near vacuum and micro-gravity which exist outside the Earth's atmosphere.

On this particular mission a range of experiments is carried. The simplest are the small cylindrical canisters anchored beneath the payload bay sill near the rear cabin bulkhead. These are Getaway Specials. The Getaway Special or GAS consists of a small, sealed canister which is switched on and off by the astronauts. They are available to anyone who can pay the fee and the only constraints are that the contents must not jeopardise flight safety, the experiment must be completely automatic and it must be of genuine scientific value.

These Getaway Specials have been marketed aggressively by NASA, illustrating the Agency's attempts to provide a space programme which has genuine accessibility for the community. The brainchild of NASA executive John Yardley, the GAS concept was sold so successfully by project engineer Gil Moore that even before the first flight of the Shuttle more than 300 had found purchasers. The fact that schools and private laboratories had to pay up to $10,000 to reserve GAS slots and willingly did so in such numbers confirms that there is a groundswell of enthusiasm for spaceflight which is waiting to be tapped.

Left:
Not only does the Space Shuttle deploy, retrieve, repair or recover satellites, but several of the missions have had scientific objectives. These missions carry a wide selection of scientific experiments and instrumentation in the payload bay or habitable areas of the Orbiter — the pallet seen here carries experiments developed by NASA's Office of Space & Terrestrial Application. The unique environment of space has opened up new areas for research in human studies, biological and physical sciences, astronomy, earth studies, etc, and the Shuttle has enabled trained scientists who are not career astronauts to spend a short time in the environment they are examining.

Right:
Scientific experiments can be carried into space by the Shuttle in a variety of ways. The experiments — in this case a Spacelab 2 configuration of solar telescopes — are located on pallets in the payload bay directly exposed to space and are controlled from the mid-deck or aft flightdeck of the Orbiter: the crew have no direct contact with the payload elements.

On a larger scale there is ample room in the Orbiter's cargo bay for scientific payloads. These can be of the fixed type, remaining in position throughout the flight, or of the free-flying type, deployed and retrieved as necessary by the RMS. Alternatively, for experiments which involve prolonged exposure to the environment of space, the LDEF can be used to carry packages in orbit for a year or more before retrieval.

On this mission the crew compartment, as well as the payload bay, has become a laboratory. Some of the most extensive research so far carried out aboard the Shuttle has been the study of space sickness or 'Space Adaptation Syndrome' (SAS), which sometimes affects astronauts (usually only on the first two or three days of a flight). On this occasion one of the Payload Specialists is acting as a guinea pig, performing a series of sharp head movements whilst wearing a blindfold. The purpose of this is to induce disorientation of the inner ear and measure the degree of sickness, if any, which results. A similar procedure has already been performed on a previous mission, with the test subject seated in a swivelling and tilting chair. On that occasion the victim vomited with abandon. (To contain this type of experiment in a weightless

cabin is not easy!) As the Commander watches the Payload Specialist attempting to make himself sick he reflects on the many different types of courage required of a spaceflight crew.

As well as human guinea pigs, real laboratory animals such as rats and monkeys have been carried aboard the Shuttle. This kind of work will continue as a normal feature of operations in the study of subjects ranging from vestibular disorientation to new surgical techniques which exploit the unique electrical characteristics of weightless cells.

For the more complex experiments a flying laboratory, Spacelab, can be carried in the cargo bay. Spacelab does not leave the bay and at present is incapable of the free flight of Skylab or the Russian Salyut (a free-flying version with solar wings has been considered). Despite this limitation Spacelab is the most versatile workshop yet to be orbited. Built in Europe by the European Space Agency, Spacelab comprises a range of options combining manned and unmanned modules. The unmanned modules are called Pallets; they are containers in which experiments are housed, to be operated remotely from within the crew compartment. Up to three Pallets can be carried.

The manned part of the Spacelab system comprises a workshop which consists either of a single module giving a modicum of working space, or of two modules sealed together to provide a much more adequate amount of room. The type of configuration, be it a Pallet only like Spacelab 2 or a mixture of manned and unmanned modules like Spacelab 1 and 3, is governed by the nature of the experiments to be flown. The first Spacelab mission (commanded by John Young) included an exotic mixture of physics and astronomy as well as numerous medical studies.

Other scientific work carried out by the Space Transportation System has ranged from the spectacular, like the bouncing of a laser beam off a mirror mounted on the Orbiter (one of the discoveries made here was that it helps to have the mirror pointed in the right direction), or the slightly dull-sounding but equally important Monodisperse Latex Reactor experiment.

The equipment carried has been equally diverse, from the 200ft long solar panel deployed by Shuttle 12 to the anonymous Getaway Specials in their canisters. Student Involvement Packages have also been carried as part of NASA's drive to involve schools and colleges with space education and give the

Above left:
Small experiments or even satellites can be carried in canisters located on the side of the payload bay. In conjunction with 'Hitchiker' payloads these help small institutes and investigators to use the environment of space in experiments which require little or no attention from a busy flight crew. Called Getaway Special Canisters (GAS), they can number over 12 on any one flight and provide easy access to space for schools, colleges and study groups, etc — hence the 'Hitchiker' name.

Above right:
The Shuttle also provides test-bed equipment and procedures to be used in orbit on later missions or programmes. During Shuttle 12 in 1984, the crew extended a 102ft solar array out of the payload bay of *Discovery* to test how the dynamic forces would affect the Shuttle or payload. Panels of this type could increase the orbital duration of Shuttle flights from the present 7-10 days to as many as 30.

space engineers of tomorrow their first taste of science in orbit.

Taken as a whole the scientific effort made possible by the Space Transportation System adds up to a huge programme of work with objectives ranging from the control of famine

Right:
Weightlessness is a great advantage in many activities, but at times it can be a disadvantage in some experiments. Several restraint devices have been tried and this one on Shuttle 5 was one of the earliest and simplest — just tape your patient to a convenient surface!

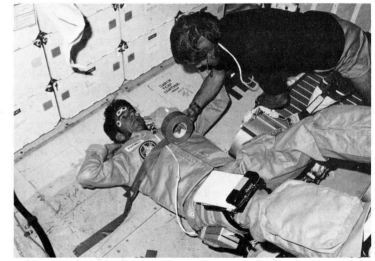

Below right:
Space Lab, Europe's contribution to the Shuttle programme, is connected to the main habitable part of the Shuttle by a tunnel. Being separated from the main living quarters it can operate in constant 12-hour shifts throughout its orbital stay, thus obtaining the maximum scientific return from each flight. In a one-week flight, two weeks worth of investigations can be made. Experiments located in the SpaceLab module are of some size but in the weightless environment of space they are easy to move. In order to facilitate operation and convenient location the equipment can be mounted on slide rails, as seen in this SpaceLab 1 photo.

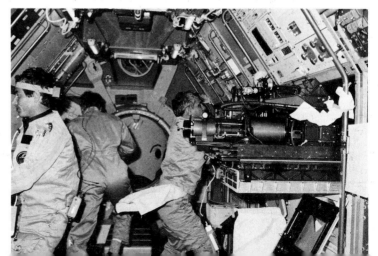

Activity on the flightdeck is fairly cramped; the mid deck below is a larger work area which enables small experiments to be located there. This Shuttle 13 photo illustrates how Payload Specialists can use the many lockers to operate small experiments and conduct observations in this area whilst the flight crew continue with other important flight activities on the flightdeck.

and the prediction of weather patterns to the combating of disease by advanced surgery and medicine. This effort is nothing new to NASA: before men were first launched into orbit it was predicted that the scientist would be the common worker of space. The use of engineering test pilots rather than pure-research scientists as the original astronauts was seen by many as a mistake, although the decision was taken at the express command of President Eisenhower in 1958.

In the event the choice of test pilots proved beneficial in the early days when the main objective of spaceflight was to test the vehicles themselves, but as early as 1963 NASA recruited two pilot-trained 'Scientist Astronauts'. In 1965 and again in 1967 entire groups of Scientist Astronauts were recruited, although it was considered necessary for these candidates to become qualified jet pilots as part of their training. Some of these scientists left the programme when, partly as a result of expenditure cuts, it became obvious that they would have to wait a very long time before they would have the opportunity of going into space.

Among those who persevered and eventually flew in orbit were Doctor Joe Allen, whose spectacular spacewalk (with Dale Gordon on Shuttle 14) to rescue two stranded satellites saved Lloyds of London £80 million, and Doctor Story Musgrave, who was EV1 on the very first Shuttle EVA. Another veteran of the 'Class of '67' was Doctor Bill Thornton who, at the age of 56, conducted medical research aboard Spacelab 3.

Perhaps the branch of science most predictably appropriate to the Space Age is astronomy. Here STS is expected to reap rich rewards by taking observations above the obscuring shield of the Earth's atmosphere. To exploit this unrestricted visibility to the full the Space Telescope has been designed. This, as its name implies, is a free-flying optical telescope which can be aimed at the stars by remote command from the ground.

Using mirrors of unprecedented quality the telescope beams its observations in digital form to astronomers on Earth. It is expected to see out to greater distances than anything yet achieved in astronomy and in so doing reveal facts about the very earliest days of the Universe. Light which started its journey across space at or near the time of the 'Big Bang' (thought to be the moment of Creation) may be detected by the powerful instruments of the Telescope; scientists may therefore be able to watch events which occurred at the dawn of time.

The working life of the Space Telescope should be at least 10 years. Despite its sophistication it is a fairly straightforward design from an engineering point of view and is self-contained, having its own power source fed by two solar panels. As the Shuttle will be able to perform maintenance and repair work in the event of a mishap there is real hope that, with this one device, the curtain will be raised on a new age of astronomy. Some have speculated that the Telescope will make the first observations of planets in orbit around other stars: although likely to exist, these planets would be too small to be seen at such great distances by ground-based optical instruments.

The scientific work of the Shuttle reflects Man's concern with the state of the planet. Earth resources monitoring from orbit may help save food supplies and limit pollution, while the study of the atmospheres of other worlds, such as Venus, may yield knowledge which will enable the eventual control (at least to some extent) of the weather. Permanent structures in space are planned as part of this effort, and the STS will make them possible. Medical experiments will help in the fight against disease and also reveal the results of long-duration spaceflight in preparation for the day when the human race starts to colonise the Solar System. Industrial processes will be improved by work in the pure environment of space, and lessons will be learned which will enable better use to be made of materials.

As the green-faced Payload Specialist completes his experiment the Commander watches sympathetically, hoping that the long-suffering scientist will remember that his discomfort is all in a good cause. On the Shuttle they are all in the same business; they are working, they hope, for a better tomorrow for the hyperactive, quarrelsome species which inhabits the blue and white globe that hangs there in the silence above the orbiting Spacecraft.

BEHIND THE SCENES

Following the delivery of an Orbiter or on completion of a mission the Orbiter is taken to the Orbiter Processing Facility next to the Vehicle Assembly Building (VAB) for preparation for its next flight. The size of the Orbiter is very evident when compared to people and vehicles around it.

Above:
As the rest of the world watches each Shuttle flight attention is drawn to the crew in space. However, like the tip of an iceberg the astronauts are but part of a vast team which supports each flight. At the forefront of the ground-based team are the controllers at

Mission Control at Houston, Texas who direct the crew and monitor and communicate with them constantly. Complementing the banks of computers are wall screens: centre is a world map indicating orbital position and ground track, and right is a Shuttle 12 screen monitoring a satellite deployment.

It is inevitable that most of the public recognition afforded to the STS programme should be focussed on the astronauts, but each Shuttle flight depends upon a huge network of specialist teams, co-ordinated by NASA but increasingly provided by private industry. It is now NASA policy to put out to tender some functions which were previously performed in-house by the Agency. An example of this is the Shuttle Processing Team, a 6,000-strong group responsible for readying the vehicle for flight. Originally an all-NASA enterprise, this function was later performed by an organisation co-ordinated by Lockheed Space Operations, a group including teams from Pan Am, Morton Thiokol (which makes the Solid Rocket Boosters) and a company headed by Apollo 13 astronaut Fred Haise called Grumman Technical Services.

The Orbiter Processing Facility (OPF) is basically a spacecraft hangar with room for two Shuttles to be processed simultaneously. The vehicle stands horizontal, surrounded by a network of walkways which allow technicians to reach every inch of the Orbiter including the belly. Two sliding platforms on movable gantries pass over the top of the Shuttle so that

work does not involve climbing on the airframe.

Processing starts with the completion of clearing-up operations following the previous flight. Tanks are drained, engine feed-pipes purged and the toilet emptied. Any damaged items are repaired or replaced and residual hardware from the recent mission is removed and the payload bay cleaned, inspected and readied for its new cargo.

The hinges of the payload bay doors are not designed for use in normal gravity: they can not therefore support the weight of the open doors on Earth. Special counterweights are used to take the load off the hinges and thus simulate zero-G.

Key to the speedy preparation of the Shuttle is the Launch Processing System, a bank of 270 computers specially programmed to 'mother' the vehicle, automatically scanning and reporting on every minute detail of the condition of its structure and systems. This facility saves manpower and also reduces the amount of clambering about which has to be done in the OPF. The traditional environment of an aircraft maintenance hangar with mechanics crawling in and out of every access

Above:
Other parts of the vehicle arrive at different times during the weeks before a flight. This is the huge External Tank arriving by ocean-going barge at Kennedy for transport to the VAB for stacking.

Below:
Now vertical inside the huge VAB, the ET is checked and mated to the Solid Rocket Boosters prior to joining the Orbiter and roll-out to the pad.

hatch with spanners in their hands would not be suitable for spacecraft processing. It is better not to touch the vehicle at all unless a computer deems it necessary, and anyone who leaves a lug-wrench behind in some part of the air-frame will not endear himself to the Shuttle's digital guardians.

Some payloads, such as Spacelab, are loaded into the cargo bay while the Shuttle is horizontal in the OPF. Other, more manageable, loads or those which need to be installed in the vertical position, are added later when the Orbiter is on the pad.

When preparations in the OPF are complete the Shuttle is towed to the Vehicle Assembly Building (VAB). Here the Solid Rocket Boosters have already been mounted on the Mobile Launch Platform (MLP). With the SRBs in place the External Tank (a new one each time, brought from the manufacturing plant at Michoud by barge up the Banana River) is attached to them. The Oribiter vehicle itself is then roated through 90° by a crane-like hoist and is mated to the ET. It is now in the upright position in which it will remain until launch.

The entire unit is then taken to the launch pad riding the Crawler, an immensely strong platform with tracked drive modules at each corner. The Crawler (the same one used to transport the Saturn Moonrocket), is the biggest land vehicle in the world, weighing more than 3,000 tons. Flat-out it can reach 2mph.

Once at the launch pad the Shuttle is surrounded by a Rotating Service Structure which enables technicians to reach any part of the spacecraft and also offers environmental

Above:
The effects of spaceflight on the Shuttle thermal protection system is evident in the loss of tiles on one of *Columbia's* OMS pods, seen between Shuttle 1 and 2 in 1981.

Below:
A detailed view of the thermal protection application on early Orbiters, with each tile numbered for identification. These tiles were gradually replaced by thermal blankets on later vehicles.

Right:
Once the payload is installed the Orbiter is mated to the ET and SRBs atop the Mobile Launch Platform then placed on the Crawler Transporter and moved the three miles to the pad.

Far right:
Once the Shuttle is on the pad the ground crew begins hours of tests and checks of not only the vehicle and its payload but also the compatibility of the vehicle and the ground support equipment. Fuel tanks are topped off and the countdown begins.

Facing page inset:
After every flight each SSME is checked and sometimes replaced with another. This photo shows the Shuttle engine installations on *Columbia* prior to Shuttle 1 in 1981.

protection to the more sensitive areas. Rain and storm damage on the pad has prompted research into ways of improving the shelter offered by the Service Structure, and it is possible that the present configuration will one day be replaced with a totally enclosed system.

Loading of the upright part of the cargo now continues and for this another purpose-built vehicle is available. This is the Vertical Payload Canister (VPC), a replica of the payload bay mounted on a self-propelled bogie. Payloads are installed in the VPC at the Cape's Vertical Processing Facility and then driven to the pad and hoisted to the desired height into the Payload Changeout Room. Here the payload is inserted into the Shuttle's cargo bay, protected all the while by a system of airtight seals so that no contamination can invade either the bay or the payload itself.

The record for Shuttle turnaround between missions stood at 54 days by the end of the programme's first five years.

Whilst preparation of the hardware is in progress other technicians, engineers and astronauts are busy with the mission's software. The digital flight plan is flown in simulation before each lift-off and it is not unknown for this check to reveal flaws in the flight's computer program. As the only sure way to check software is to run it, this part of the preparation is vital. The scene for this crucial activity is the Shuttle Avionics Integration Laboratory or SAIL, a building which contains a full scale Orbiter mock-up and flight simulator. Astronauts man the 'Orbiter' during full mission simulations and, as well as the routine elements of the planned flight, any number of emergencies or alternative procedures can be examined. The normal method is not to fly a mission from start to finish (although this is possible) but to study each particular segment of the flight in isolation, examining alternatives and possible problems at the same time. In this way an in-depth knowledge of every part of the mission sequence is developed rather than an overall view.

The SAIL includes not only the Orbiter and its equipment, such as the RMS Arm, but also simulated payloads so that Prox Ops can be practised against images of satellites thrown

Above:
The relaxed nature of T-shirt training is evident on the mock-up flightdeck of the Shuttle as these four astronauts train for Shuttle 7.

Below:
For training on the MMU the astronauts use a 'flying simulator' to practise manoeuvring the MMU around objects. In this training shot 'Solar Max' approaches.

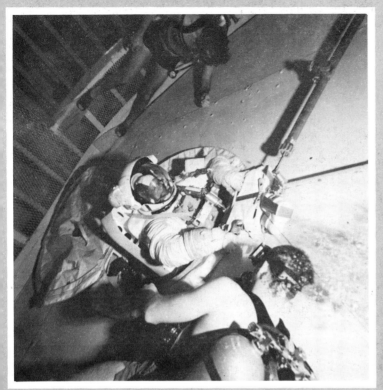

against the simulator screens. Full re-entry can also be simulated along with abort procedures, and in the event of any serious error on the part of the astronaut the Orbiter can even be crashed for complete realism! It is little wonder that a session in the SAIL can be as exhausting an experience as a genuine flight.

Astronauts also undertake other training specific to each mission. EVA spacewalkers practise in a water tank, carrying out the full planned EVA in simulated microgravity using the same equipment to be used in space. Payload Specialists are trained in the intricacies of their own experiments and may spend long periods at the manufacturer's plant. Mission Specialists simulate the necessary Prox Ops and procedures for satellite deployment and retrieval (for example) and attend lengthy briefings on the flight's objectives which may include an appreciation of several disciplines such as astronomy, medicine and geology. As scientists and engineers themselves, the Mission Specialists may play a key role in the planning of the flight and the design of its special equipment.

Not only the crew needs preparation: the support personnel at Kennedy Spaceflight Center and Mission Control, Houston, also practise detailed simulations of the mission, and at the Payload Operation Control Centers the payload-specific aspects of the flight are studied. In the event of problems with any payload, the decisions at these Centres could be vital.

As another mission nears its conclusion the Commander of the orbiting Shuttle reflects on all this effort which has enabled the flight plan to be carried out so successfully. With the main objectives achieved the Capcom at Mission Control allows himself a little time for congratulation:

'Looks like you guys have done a fine job today'.

The Commander thanks him for the remark, and adds:

'And we would like to thank all the people on the ground for looking after us, and for all the hard work that has gone into this mission'.

His words may sound like a simple politeness, but they are more than that: they express a genuine emotion which every astronaut feels and which few find easy to describe.

READY FOR ANYTHING

The key to safety aboard the Space Shuttle is preparation. Something goes wrong on every flight, and it is a well-known saying among astronauts that each mission carries an extra crew member: 'Murphy'. The answer therefore is not simply to prevent as many mishaps as possible, but to be ready for them when they do occur.

On the launch pad the most obvious hazard is an explosion. A quick evacuation from the vehicle is possible although if the White Room had already been retracted the astronauts would have to wait until it was replaced. Once out of the Orbiter they would run along the Crew Access Arm to the Support Tower and ride slidewires to the ground.

Fire is another ever-present danger. The Shuttle carries a sophisticated fire detection and suppression system which operates during every phase of the mission including on the pad before lift-off. Smoke detectors are placed strategically throughout the entire cabin and an automatic system of fixed-position extinguishers is backed up by hand-held extinguishers within easy reach of the crew. If the oxygen in the Life Support System is threatened by fire the pressure of the cabin atmosphere can be reduced to a low enough level to inhibit the spread of flame while still maintaining survivable conditions for the crew. In such cases a reserve oxygen supply is available, and if necessary the astronauts can evacuate the craft using EMUs and Personal Rescue Spheres to transfer to a rescue ship or to wait until conditions aboard their own vehicle improve.

Left:
Despite excellent work by the astronauts in space and support teams on the ground, not all EVAs go according to plan. Following the failure of a satellite (released from Shuttle 16 in 1985) to activate itself, plans were made to attempt to activate the timing sequencer during the same flight that launched it. EVA was a part of this planning and involved the crew attaching activation devices to the RMS end effector, as this photo shows.

Emergencies during the lift-off and ascent phase can be countered with the various Abort options. Once in orbit perhaps the most difficult problem to anticipate would be a medical one, as the body is less predictable than machinery. Minor illnesses have been successfully treated in space, but their effects can be complex. Nausea can cause dehydration and weakness while a cold is misery in weightlessness because the sinuses are unable to drain in the normal manner. Colds can also endanger the eardrums if rapid pressure changes are experienced on a mission.

The Shuttle carries a medical kit which includes equipment for serious injuries, for example an intravenous drip. Most orthopaedic injuries could be treated at least until an emergency re-entry enabled the patient to be taken to hospital.

During EVA the obvious hazards of suit malfunction are countered by the display panel which monitors oxygen levels and other safety points. A serious mishap during EVA would be failure of the MMU at some distance from the Orbiter. Tracking equipment is carried to reveal the astronaut's position and facilitate rescue.

The total failure of the de-orbit manoeuvre is unlikely, as even with both OMS engines not working a retrofire could be achieved by a long firing of the RCS thrusters against the line of flight. Once re-entry has started there is less margin for accidents. The angle of entry has to be exactly right and this is achieved automatically. If the digital autopilot failed a manual approach would be virtually impossible. Such a problem would be revealed in the checks prior to re-entry, however, and the de-orbit would be delayed until the problem was cured.

In the event of a ditching or crash landing the Shuttle crew has enough survival equipment to last out until rescued (even in a remote area, although remote area survival training has been curtailed). Perhaps the greatest hazard after a crash landing would be injury from the Orbiter itself, as the whole airframe would be very hot from aerodynamic friction. A thermal blanket is carried in the cabin, which would be thrown across the side of the vehicle before an exit could be attempted.

From launch to landing, therefore, the planning tries to cover every contingency. The first five years of the Shuttle programme produced a range of problems of varying seriousness. It would be impractical to record here every snag which occurred during those 25 flights, but the following summary illustrates the kind of events which posed a threat to the successful accomplishment of a mission.

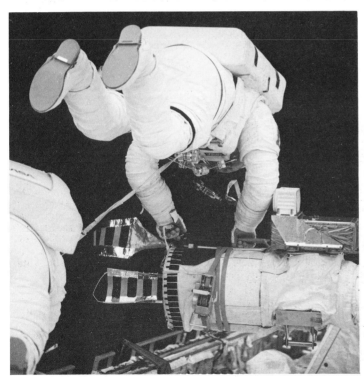

Left:
Astronauts Hoffman (above) and Griggs (left) attached two trip devices to the RMS which were formed from flight documentation files and tape and secured by payload retention straps. The EVA lasted about three hours.

Following the attempts of Mission Specialist Seddon to snag the lever on the satellite the crew evaluated their efforts on the 'fly swatters'. The switch on the satellite did move but did not activate the satellite as planned. The RMS was not used again during the mission so there was no further EVA to remove them. A later EVA was planned to repair the still faulty satellite.

Shuttle 1 — Orbital Flight Test 1 — *Columbia* 1

Heatshield tiles were ripped away by aerodynamic forces during launch. This posed a threat to safe atmospheric re-entry when the heatshield provides vital protection against the fireball which results from skin friction. To some extent the crew was prepared for this eventuality, having practised (in the simulator) using the angle of bank during landing approach to dissipate heat from specific areas of the airframe, but it was still worrying that tile damage had occurred on the very first flight.

This followed extensive trouble-shooting on the tiles which had delayed the programme by two years. With hindsight it is perhaps not surprising that the tiles suffered some setbacks, for the Shuttle's Thermal Protection System is a true miracle of technology. The tiles are made from ultra-pure Silica fibres (basically a type of glass) which conduct heat so poorly that it is possible to heat a TPS tile or 'brick' until its centre is as hot as the surface of the sun, and then pick it up with bare hands. The heat trapped in the tile takes so long to radiate out to the surface that the corners of the tile remain cool to the touch.

As the function of the tiles is to protect the aluminium structure of the Shuttle from heat it is necessary for them to fit perfectly to the contours of the vehicle. Each tile is individually designed for a specific location and is manufactured by its own computer program. Recycling the program produces an identical tile.

To enable the structure of the Orbiter to flex in flight (as all aircraft do) the tiles are mounted on special felt material which allows them the necessary freedom of movement. (Thermal blankets, later used on *Discovery* and *Atlantis* to replace some tiles, more easily accommodate this flexing.)

In the event, Shuttle 1 returned safely despite the lost tiles, but there were to be further TPS problems throughout the early flights.

Shuttle 2 — OFT 2 — *Columbia* 2

Fuel cell malfunctions caused this planned five day flight to be reduced to a 'minimum mission' and the Shuttle was brought home after only two days.

Shuttle 3 — OFT 3 — *Columbia* 3

After problems with the toilet, with crew sickness and with APUs and communications, high winds in the landing area caused a postponement of the re-entry. The Shuttle always has life support in hand for such an eventuality and the number of possible landing sites makes it unlikely that a return could not be made before oxygen and food ran out.

Shuttle 4 — OFT 4 — *Columbia* 4

After a lightning strike on the pad two days before launch this mission began with the loss of the two SRBs, due to the premature firing of explosive bolts which separated the boosters from their parachutes. The rockets hit the water at high speed and sank 3,500ft to the bottom (one was later recovered). Meanwhile the Orbiter itself was in trouble: at launch no one realised that hail damage to the TPS had enabled rainwater to penetrate the protective layer of tiles. The subsequent out-gassing of water vapour in orbit was a problem not only in relation to the heatshield but also due to the forces of the out-gassing which acted like a thruster to disrupt navigation and attitude control. This was cured by reprogramming the DAP. Later, during landing approach, chase pilots could see the vapour streaming back from the Shuttle's wings.

An even more exotic potential hazard occurred when the Shuttle passed within eight miles of a spent Soviet booster (without seeing it). Space is a big enough place for the danger of a collision to be small . . . at the moment. Radar could well give an adequate warning of the presence of large space flotsam, although a meteor might present a more serious hazard.

Shuttle 5 — Mission 31A — *Columbia* 5

On this, the first operational flight of STS, the planned EVA was postponed due to space sickness and then cancelled altogether when both EMU suits malfunctioned (the astronauts were suited-up in the airlock when this happened). Good discipline prevented injury.

At the end of the flight another mishap occurred when a wheel locked during the landing roll-out. Although this was not serious, any undercarriage malfunction is worrying as the gear, once extended, cannot be recycled. It is one of the few systems on the Shuttle which has no backup (although a belly landing would be survivable).

Shuttle 6 — 32B — *Challenger* 1

Challenger's first flight suffered long delays due to engine problems. Once launched, as well as TPS blanket damage during ascent, there was a moment of anxiety during the EVA (the first of the STS programme). An EMU suit registered an oxygen alarm, suggesting that oxygen was being consumed too quickly. Over-exertion was the cause and the alarm enabled the danger to be surmounted.

Shuttle 7 — 31C — *Challenger* 2
One of the three APUs which provide hydraulic power for the control surfaces malfunctioned in orbit. During the normal checkout of the controls on the day before re-entry the unit underspeeded and then shut down. As an elevon control is vital to the landing approach the fault was serious and ruled out a suggested delay (due to bad weather) of the return. In the event the APU worked satisfactorily during the recovery.

Indirectly this incident focused attention on the availability of alternative landing sites when poor weather hits Kennedy and Edwards. During launch of Shuttle 7, Runway 15 at KSC had been closed by rain, so that an abort would have offered only one landing option, Runway 33 (the same runway but approached from the opposite end).

At the end of this mission the planned landing at Kennedy Spaceflight Center was cancelled in favour of Edwards Air Force Base, California (a landing ground preferred by most Shuttle pilots due to less critical weather parameters). Possible ways to add further landing options which were studied after this mission included the establishment of alternative sites at Homestead Air Force Base (Miami), Cherry Point Marine Air Station (North Carolina) and Orlando Airport (Florida), as well as the possibility of extending the apron of the Orbiter tow-way leading to the VAB at Kennedy to provide a high-speed turn-off from Runway 15.

Shuttle 8 — 31D — *Challenger* 3
During the first two minutes of ascent an SRB booster nozzle came close to structural failure. It just managed to hold out; if it had not there could have been a disaster. Later in the flight the RMS Arm, fitted with a TV camera, was used to survey the Shuttle's belly tiles, demonstrating that it is possible to examine inaccessible parts without an EVA.

Shuttle 9/Spacelab 1 — 41A — *Columbia* 6
A heavy workload caused irritability among the Spacelab 1 crew. Before the space age, science fiction writers made much of the psychological dangers of spaceflight such as emotional stress in the claustrophobic confines of a spaceship. In reality it has been demonstrated that a cool and competent

Commander is the only remedy needed. In this case the Commander was the incomparable John Young so there was no problem at all.

Recovery of the SRBs from the sea revealed a more tangible threat. Shrapnel from explosive bolts fired during the separation of the boosters was embedded in the sides of the rockets. The danger that other fragments had struck the Orbiter belly tiles, damaging the heatshield, was obvious. In fact the TPS functioned perfectly on landing approach. The mission's problems were not over, however. Having suffered a computer failure prior to re-entry, *Columbia* experienced a fire which broke out at the rear of the craft during the let-down to the runway. This was not noticed until after touchdown and was of a minor nature.

Shuttle 10 — 41B — *Challenger* 4
This involved highly publicised failures, those of the PAM units attached to satellites Westar 6 and Palapa B2. The first flight of the MMU restored the dignity of the mission and NASA later retrieved the satellites with a spectacular rescue flight. Shuttle 10 also suffered RMS problems, always worrying in view of the safety role of the Arm.

Shuttle 11 — 41C — *Challenger* 5
An attempt to repair a fuse on the MMS satellite Solar Max with a spacewalk ran into difficulties and the objective was eventually achieved with use of the RMS Arm. Although the EVA problems were disappointing the ability of STS to carry out repairs in space was demonstrated, with important safety implications.

Shuttle 12 — 41D — *Discovery* 1
A launch cancellation with the crew already on board was followed by a Redundant Set Launch Sequencer (RSLS) abort which shut down the engines within three seconds of firing. Residual hydrogen then caught fire, scorching the Orbiter's body flap. Two days later came another cancellation.

After an eventual delay of two months the mission was ready to go again. This time a light aircraft intruded into the Cape Canaveral airspace and held up the lift-off. When finally the Shuttle blasted into space the flight proved an overall success although an icicle which blocked the toilet waste outlet had to be removed with the RMS Arm (earning the crew the nickname 'Ice Busters').

Shuttle 13 — 41G — *Challenger* 6

Communications were the problem on this mission with the TDRS satellite off the air for 11 hours due to a fault. In the event of loss of ground communication the flight can continue safely as all flight plan objectives are achievable with onboard software. This includes the re-entry and landing phase, (although TDRS would not be needed during this phase anyway).

Shuttle 14 — 51A — *Discovery* 2

High winds delayed the launch and in orbit the helmet lights on the astronauts' EMU suits failed. These lights are not essential and no remedial action was necessary. This was a satellite rescue mission and when the satellites failed to fit into the planned supports, manhandling them into the payload bay proved so arduous that one of the spacewalkers wore through a layer of insulation on his suit gloves.

Shuttle 15 — 51C — *Discovery* 3

Ice on the launch pad caused concern at the start of the mission; and at the very end, during the landing roll, carbon dust was clearly visible from the brakes. Although not critical this served as a reminder of the stresses involved in landing a 100-ton vehicle at 180kt.

Shuttle 16 — 51D Revised — *Discovery* 4

Even NASA's flair for improvisation does not always work. In this case a 'flyswatter' device was made from the cut-up cover of a flight manual in order to trip a switch on a faulty satellite. The device was attached to the RMS end-effector (during the first unscheduled EVA of the programme) and it did throw the switch as planned, but the satellite still wouldn't operate. A burst tyre on landing added insult but not injury.

Shuttle 17 — 51B — *Challenger* 7

A medical experiment was threatened when a monkey refused to eat. A pep talk restored the animal's appetite, but the question remains whether the unpredictability of animals presents any hazard on laboratory type flights. Restraints limit the risk of any material damage, but the danger of infection is more real. The medical space programme is so important that the use of animals is bound to increase significantly. One safety improvement might be to enable a Spacelab crew to remain in the laboratory module during launch and re-entry, thus guarding the flightcrew against possible contamination. With major modification this might be possible.

Shuttle 18 — 51G — *Discovery* 5

A smooth launch followed a day of bad weather during which the pad was struck by lightning. This flight was a great success but suffered a moment of embarrassment when scientists on Earth tried to bounce a laser beam off a mirror mounted on the Orbiter. An error had resulted in the Shuttle being positioned so that the mirror was on the side facing away from Earth. Another positioning difficulty was experienced by Arabsat Payload Specialist Prince Sultan Salman Al-Saud, a Moslem. Praying to Mecca proved difficult with the ground streaking by at 17,000mph, and Mission Control passed him special co-ordinates to enable him to face in the right direction at the right time.

Shuttle 19 — 51F — *Challenger* 8

This saw the first Abort to Orbit, when the centre main engine failed during the ascent. Three and a half minutes after lift-off, with the Shuttle at 9,000mph, the engine started to overheat and was shut down. If this had happened 33 seconds earlier a forced landing at Saragossa, Spain, would have been inevitable. A second engine then showed signs of overheating and for a moment it seemed that this too would be shut down, necessitating a landing at Crete. The Commander decided, however, that the sensors were exaggerating and overruled the computer so that the second engine kept running. Some 4,000lb of fuel was burnt off with the OMS engines to lighten the ship and a safe orbit was achieved, proving that the Commander's judgement had been correct when he disconnected the heat sensor.

This dramatic abort did not prevent the mission being flown almost as planned, with great scientific benefits.

Shuttle 20 — 51I — *Discovery* 6

After launch delays due to the need to replace a back-up computer the mission climbed out through a gap in heavy cloud. Once in orbit there was a temporary problem when a sunshield snagged one of the payload satellites. The satellite was unhitched by the RMS, despite a failure which prevented the Arm from being used in the computer assisted mode. Later in the mission a satellite-rescue EVA was carried out, proving yet again that even when things go wrong they can often be put right.

Above:
Four months later, in August 1985, Shuttle 20 approached the Leasat satellite in a second attempt to activate it. Astronaut van Hoften is seen here on the end of the RMS prior to grasping the satellite and manually slowing it down to attach retention bars on to it for a subsequent 'jump-lead' repair of a faulty electrical circuit. Once it had been captured, astronaut Bill Fisher worked at the side of the satellite attaching the electrical bypass system to allow ground controllers to activate the satellite some weeks after the astronauts had returned home.

Above:
The repairs completed, astronaut van Hoften strikes a Charles Atlas pose after manually spinning up the satellite and casting it adrift in space. He appears to be holding the world on his shoulders.

Below:
The faces of Lounge and Covey peer from the aft flightdeck windows at the end of the Shuttle 20 EVA. A spectacular view of Earth behind the crew above the roof of *Discovery* completes the picture; note also the thermal blanketing of the surfaces of the Shuttle.

Shuttle 21 — 51J — *Atlantis* 1

Information restricted due to military nature of flight.

Shuttle 22 — 61A — *Challenger* 9

Two experiments failed during the mission but were salvaged by in-flight repair in the classic NASA tradition of improvisation.

Shuttle 23 — 61B — *Atlantis* 2

Fog at Edwards Air Force Base almost forced the delay of re-entry. In the event the Shuttle returned through marginal weather, breaking cloud a mere 5,000ft over the Mojave Desert (lower than on any other shuttle flight).

Shuttle 24 — 61C — *Columbia* 7

Planned re-entry thruster firing tests were cancelled when, by chance, it was discovered by ground technicians that an explosion in the nose of the Orbiter could result. A night landing at Edwards followed, after bad weather cancelled the planned return to Kennedy Spaceflight Center.

Shuttle 25 — 51L — *Challenger* 10

The first five years of STS ended in tragedy when *Challenger* exploded 72 seconds after launch (the first from the newly-refurbished Pad 39B) on Tuesday 28 January 1986. The explosion occurred at 47,000ft (14,326m) altitude, eight miles (12.8km) down-range from Cape Canaveral.

Meticulous crash investigation revealed that the probable cause of the explosion was the failure of the right SRB, which ruptured and then broke loose from its mounting, puncturing the ET and causing the fuel inside to detonate. It was argued that excessively cold pre-launch temperatures contributed to the accident (*Challenger* had been on the pad for a month, enduring frequent rain and freezing conditions). It would be impossible to describe adequately the intricacies of the investigation within the scope of this book. Suffice it to say that, at a tragic and totally unacceptable cost, lessons were learned which will make space-flight safer throughout the rest of man's history. This fact is the only worthy memorial to the astronauts who gave their lives.

THE CHALLENGER DISASTER

This table of events, together with their most likely interpretation, has been compiled with reference to detailed analyses of NASA records.

Time	Speaker	Event
T	Resnik:	'All right'
+½sec	—	Puff of black smoke visible from rear of right SRB, evidence of failure of joint seal between booster segments.
+1sec	Smith:	'Here we go'
+7sec	Scobee:	'Houston, *Challenger* roll programme'
+11sec	Smith:	'Go, you mother'
+12sec	—	Completion of roll programme, further sighting of black smoke (visible on film but not to crew or to naked eye).
+14sec	Resnik:	'LVLH' (This is a routine statement indicating that the Attitude Direction Indicator is set to provide Local Vertical/Local Horizontal or LVLH.)
+15sec	Resnik:	'Shit hot' (This is a common expression amongst crews indicating that things appear to be going very well.)
+16sec	Scobee:	'Ooohkaaaay'
+19sec	Smith:	'Looks like we've got a lot of wind here today'
+20sec	Scobee:	'Yeah' Main engines now throttle to 94% as normal.
+22sec	Scobee:	'It's a little hard to see out my window here'
+28sec	Smith:	'There's 10,000 feet and Mach point 5'
+35sec	Scobee:	'Point 9'
+36sec	—	Main engines now throttle to 65% as normal.
+40sec	Smith:	'There's Mach 1' At this point *Challenger* encounters a wind shear; it is possible, but not certain, that this may have increased the stress on the damaged SRB.
+41sec	Scobee:	'Going through 19,000 (feet)'
+43sec	Scobee:	'Okay, we're throttling down'
+57sec	Scobee:	'Throttling up'
+58sec	Smith:	'Throttle up' Smoke is now seen again by the tracking cameras and appears to be in the area of the failed seal.
+59sec	Scobee:	'Roger' The point of maximum dynamic pressure ('MaxQ') has now been reached (702lb/sq ft). The SRB is now probably unable to withstand stresses. Flame is now visible from damaged joint.
+1min	Smith:	'Feel that mother go'
	(?):	'Woohoo!' More flame becomes visible and SRB thrust chamber pressures become divergent.

+1m, 2s	Smith:	'35,000 (feet) going through 1 point 5 (Mach)'
+1m, ½s	—	Right outboard elevon moved by auto command; main engine gimballing occurs and vehicle pitches slightly. These events are all thought to have been a reaction to winds, not the failed SRB.
+1m, 5s	Scobee:	'Reading 486 on mine'
+1m, 6s	—	Fire now visible at top of SRB on side facing Orbiter.
+1m, 6½s	—	ET Liquid Hydrogen pressure begins to deviate.
+1m, 7s	Smith:	'Yep, that's what I've got too' Rate of increase of engine Liquid Oxygen inlet pressure slows at completion of throttling back up to 104% power.
+1m, 10s	Scobee:	'Roger, GO at throttle-up'
+1m, 12s	—	Vehicle is nudged sideways towards the failed SRB at 0.227g. Lower right SRB attach points fail (either from flame damage or due to aerodynamic forces caused by the outgassing from the failed seal acting as a rogue 'thruster'). SRB then separates from lower attach point; lower end of booster moves outward, pivoting top end towards ET.

At the same time the SRB lower end pitches upwards towards right wing of Orbiter which it may have severed at this moment, as well as damaging the rear of the fuselage with flame efflux. Spacecraft yaws to the left at 0.254g. SSME Liquid Oxygen/Liquid Hydrogen inlet pressures drop, evidence that ET is now ruptured (by pivoting top end of SRB).

+1m, 13s	Smith:	'Uh-oh' Right SRB chamber pressure now 24lb/sq in below that of left SRB. Transmission of data (via upper SRB attach point) continues, indicating that upper attach point still intact.

Bottom of ET blows out, acting like a rocket and ramming the tank forward with a thrust of 2.8 million pounds which destroys front section of ET. Escaping gas is visible from ET as well as fire under the Orbiter, near the nose area. As ET explodes, data continues to be transmitted. Near Mach 2 at 48,000ft the engines exceed design limits, and Number 1 engine shuts down a moment before all data is lost at T+73.605 seconds.

Challenger then broke up, due to aerodynamic stress. It is thought that the forces experienced by the crew at this point would have been between 12 and 20g, and would have fallen within 10 seconds to less than 4g. These forces are not violent enough to be fatal. Cameras showed the now wingless Orbiter emerging from the fireball with Nitrogen Tetroxide spilling from its ruptured Reaction Control System. The crew module, severed from the main body of the fuselage, continued in an upward arc for 25 seconds, reaching 65,000ft before free-falling to the sea. The IUS payload was also seen emerging intact from the explosion, along with the cluster of SSMEs which were still firing on the fuel residue in the feed pipes. The colour of the SSME efflux indicated that an oxygen-rich shut-down was in progress.

The SRBs continued to ascend under their own power until range safety officers destroyed them by radio command at T+1 minute 50 seconds.

The crew module hit the water at 207mph, 2 minutes 45 seconds after the disintegration of *Challenger*. Examination of the wreckage revealed that some of the crew's Personal Egress Air Packs (PEAPs) had been activated, indicating that members of the crew had remained conscious for at least some seconds after the explosion. The PEAPs are mounted on the side of Mission and Payload Specialists' seats, but on the backs of the seats of the Commander and Pilot (therefore being impossible to activate unless the Commander/Pilot leaves the seat). The fact that Pilot Smith's PEAP was found to have been activated suggests that Judy Resnik managed to lean forward and activate it, as well as her own PEAP.

Consumption of air from the packs was, in at least one case, consistent with breathing being maintained throughout the time of the fall to the ocean. Although it is therefore likely that at least one crew member was alive at the moment of impact with the water, it is very unlikely that anyone aboard remained conscious for more than 15 seconds following the explosion, as the PEAP is not a pressure breathing device and therefore the (likely) loss of cabin pressure at altitude would cause unconsciousness due to hypoxia.

The impact with the ocean caused severe damage which destroyed the evidence of whether or not a high altitude decompression had occurred. For similar reasons the cause of death of the crew was 'not positively determined', according to the chief medical investigator, former Skylab astronaut Dr Joe Kerwin.

COMING HOME

The mission is now approaching its conclusion. The satellite launches have been achieved, Earth observations carried out, medical experiments conducted and a satellite repaired. The last item on the worklist is a meticulous clean-up of the Orbiter crew compartment, scheduled for the next-to-last full day of the flight. The last full day is kept clear of major tasks if possible, to allow the crew to rest in preparation for the re-entry and also to build some slack into the Task/Time line so that there will be a margin for dealing with any unforeseen events. This clean-up involves more than simply a natural pride in a smart ship: unstowed objects floating in zero gravity may become dangerous as they regain their weight during atmospheric re-entry.

A week in orbit generates a lot of garbage. This waste is collected in large bags which are stowed in the airlock, which now becomes a giant trash can. Some waste may be dumped overboard but NASA tries to be a good neighbour in space if possible. The crew replace and reconfigure their seats ready for the de-orbit manoeuvre.

Great concentration is also needed at Mission Control where vital data must be monitored before a 'Go' is given for the return.

The clean-up proceeds without trouble and eventually the last day dawns, allowing a brief respite from the intense activity before what is perhaps the most critical phase of the mission.

Below:
In orbit, the crew has completed its programme and prepares for the return home. This is the time for final photographs for the family album, with an over-dressed gate-crasher behind.

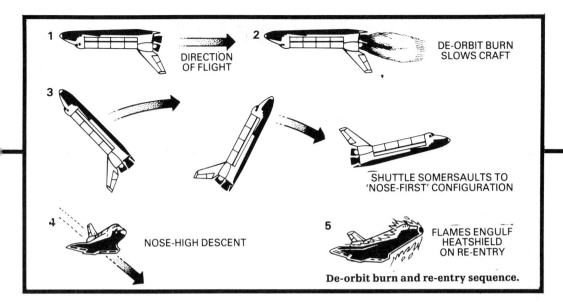

1 DIRECTION OF FLIGHT

2 DE-ORBIT BURN SLOWS CRAFT

3 SHUTTLE SOMERSAULTS TO 'NOSE-FIRST' CONFIGURATION

4 NOSE-HIGH DESCENT

5 FLAMES ENGULF HEATSHIELD ON RE-ENTRY

De-orbit burn and re-entry sequence.

There has, on this occasion, been no great alteration to the flight plan, and so the final full day contains nothing more arduous than a press conference by television down-link.

At the last minute a change of plan is announced. Storms are lashing the coast at Kennedy, and the landing ground is switched to Edwards Air Force Base, California. The Commander acknowledges the alteration. Then the final sleep period comes. The Commander sleeps well, and to wake him Houston jokingly plays a tape which dates from earlier in his career:

'Rise and shine, it's Splashdown day!'

The Capcom adds: 'Please delete "Splashdown" and insert "Touchdown"!'

Now follows a series of vital actions, perhaps the most fundamental of which is to close the payload bay doors. It would be completely impossible for the Shuttle to re-enter the atmosphere with these open, as the interior of the Cargo Bay is not protected by the Thermal Protection System. It would therefore be incinerated and the aerodynamic drag of the open doors would stress the vehicle beyond limits, causing break-up.

The closure of the doors is therefore essential and if the automatic systems fail the doors can be cranked shut manually. Astronauts are trained to do this (an EVA is needed) in the water tank at Huntsville where weightlessness can be simulated.

Mission Control 'You are Go for payload bay door closing.'

From the windows of the Aft Crew Station the

doors can be seen moving gently back to the closed configuration. Darkness returns to the payload bay.

Commander 'Confirm the doors are closed.'

By the time the crew return to their seats the landing is only two hours away. The crew check the Reaction Control System and load the de-orbit flightplan into the computer. After the burn a separate code for 'pre-entry coast' will be selected.

The auxiliary power units must also be started to provide power for the flight controls during the atmospheric stage of the descent.

Commander 'APU pre-start complete.'

Before the OMS engines can be fired against the line of flight to slow the Shuttle from its orbital speed and thus cause re-entry, the vehicle must be turned around to fly 'tail first'.

Mission Control 'We are 30 seconds from loss of signal. You have a preliminary Go for the burn.'

As the Shuttle passes out of range of the Bermuda relay station work continues on the flightdeck. After 8½ minutes Ascension Island establishes communication.

Mission Control 'Start to manoeuvre to Burn attitude when convenient.'

The Reaction Control System is now used to turn the Shuttle through 180°. Houston monitors the manoeuvre by telemetry.

Mission Control 'Your Burn attitude looks good. You are Go for de-orbit burn, loss of

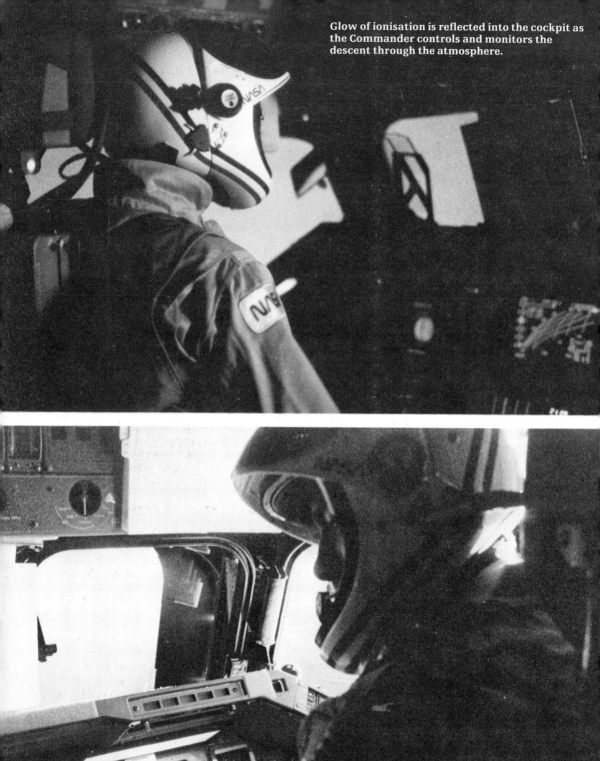

Glow of ionisation is reflected into the cockpit as the Commander controls and monitors the descent through the atmosphere.

During re-entry the pilot reads trajectory data from one of three cathode ray tubes on the flightdeck.

signal in 30 seconds, Botswana in five minutes.'

The crew now carry out a single APU start and arm the OMS engines ready for the retrofire. While still out of touch with the ground they punch into the computer the command which will initiate the firing. At the rear of the Orbiter the OMS engines ignite; they burn for three minutes.

The ignition itself is not usually felt as more than a gentle nudge, but on this occasion, as on Shuttle 9, there is a 'hard light' which sends a judder throughout the ship. The Commander glances at the pilot beside him, who seems unconcerned. The actual deceleration of the vehicle is quite imperceptible.

Engine checks follow the burn and then a pitch manoeuvre is initiated to turn the Shuttle once more into a nose-first attitude for the re-entry. The ship somersaults gracefully at 17,000mph until a 30° angle of attack is reached. The Orbiter is now fully committed to a fall into the atmosphere.

Commander 'We had a good burn on time. Residuals were three tenths.'

With the vehicle in the correct attitude the remaining propellants in the forward RCS have been dumped and a careful re-entry alignment is made to ensure that the vehicle is in the precise attitude at which the TPS tiles on the nose and undersides will bear the full brunt of the frictional heat of the descent. This alignment must be completely accurate and is very hard to achieve, a fact which has saved the lives of many people in Europe, although they probably don't know it: the wartime V2 rocket, which did not have the benefit of NASA's computers, often re-entered the lower atmosphere sideways and disintegrated harmlessly at high altitude.

Commander 'We have two out of three APUs up and running, that's nominal.'

He checks the attitude indications, and notices an anomaly.

Commander 'We have a miscorrelation with the attitude reading on the inertial ball; I'm going to centre the needles manually.'

Mission Control 'We agree with that.'

The shuttle hits the atmosphere at 400,000ft (121,920m) altitude, 5,000 miles (8,047km) from the destination runway. It was at Edwards, almost 30 years ago, that the Commander began his career as a test pilot, and where the X-15 and the other rocketplanes which sired

the Shuttle wrote history in the sky. Now Edwards is preparing to recover the hottest rocketplane of all.

As the Orbiter falls belly-first into the upper reaches of the atmosphere its speed has decreased by 1,000mph to approximately 16,500mph (26,553km/hr). Frictional heating now begins and the Thermal Protection System operates as a heat sink to spread the tremendous temperature stresses over the tiled TPS surface, parts of which will reach 2,750°F (1,510°C). The heat builds up until it is so intense that the air surrounding the descending vehicle ionises, forming a plasma wave which electrically insulates the Shuttle from all radio communication. During this blackout no messages or telemetry signals can pass between the Orbiter and Mission Control.

This critical phase of the flight begins approximately 25 minutes before landing and lasts for 12 minutes during which the Commander, Pilot and onboard computer bear full responsibility for the safe return of the spacecraft and its occupants.

On the ground observers await the first sighting of the Shuttle. The vehicle is now so hot that ozone molecules in the air are disrupted. They combine with nitric oxide molecules to form nitrogen dioxide, and in so doing create a vivid orange glow which streaks back from the Spacecraft in a comet-like trail.

As the blackout period begins the Commander de-activates the RCS roll thrusters. The forward RCS jets are now useless, inhibited by the aerodynamic forces of re-entry, but the aft jets remain effective and are used until the vehicle is at a speed and altitude at which the control surfaces will operate. The transition from RCS to aerodynamic control is made gradually. The roll thrusters are switched off when a dynamic pressure of 10lb/sq ft is reached and the elevons take over to control the all-important angle of bank (which is used to even out the structural heating and the rate of descent). This occurs at about 300,000ft (91,440m).

About two minutes later a dynamic pressure of 20lb/sq in is indicated and the pitch thrusters hand over to the elevons. At the climax of the blackout, with wing leading edges at 2,732°F (1,500°C), the crew prepares to initiate the first of a series of S turns or roll reversals which will keep the Shuttle's kinetic energy within limits as it approaches the runway.

Despite the heat outside, the shirt-sleeve environment on board is still preserved except that the astronauts are once again wearing

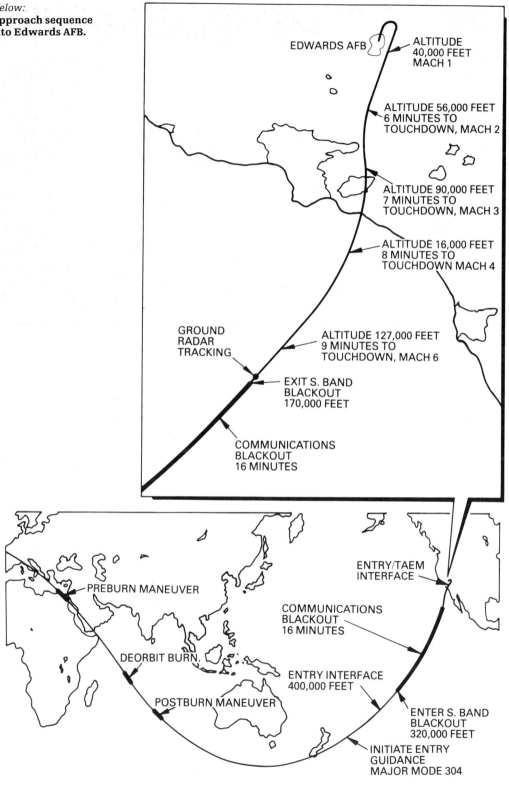

Below:
Approach sequence into Edwards AFB.

EDWARDS AFB

ALTITUDE 40,000 FEET MACH 1

ALTITUDE 56,000 FEET 6 MINUTES TO TOUCHDOWN, MACH 2

ALTITUDE 90,000 FEET 7 MINUTES TO TOUCHDOWN, MACH 3

ALTITUDE 16,000 FEET 8 MINUTES TO TOUCHDOWN MACH 4

GROUND RADAR TRACKING

ALTITUDE 127,000 FEET 9 MINUTES TO TOUCHDOWN, MACH 6

EXIT S. BAND BLACKOUT 170,000 FEET

COMMUNICATIONS BLACKOUT 16 MINUTES

PREBURN MANEUVER

DEORBIT BURN

POSTBURN MANEUVER

ENTRY/TAEM INTERFACE

COMMUNICATIONS BLACKOUT 16 MINUTES

ENTRY INTERFACE 400,000 FEET

ENTER S. BAND BLACKOUT 320,000 FEET

INITIATE ENTRY GUIDANCE MAJOR MODE 304

Above:
The Shuttle makes a remarkably steep approach to the landing strip. This is Landing Strip 22 at Edwards AFB visible from the cockpit during the final approach of *Challenger*.

Above right:
At final line-up the strip looks dauntingly short. With no power for an overshoot, the Shuttle has to be landed first time.

their lightweight helmets. On early test flights of the Orbiter when ejection seats were fitted, crew escape was possible on the approach below 100,000ft (30,480m). Now that the Shuttle has become operational the only method of return to Earth is in the vehicle itself.

After the first roll reversal the Orbiter emerges from the ionisation blackout. The Commander is initiating the second S turn when he hears Houston calling into his headset.

Commander 'Read you loud and clear.'

The aerodynamic speed brake on the vertical tail fin is now fully deployed, increasing the vehicle's profile drag and slowing it down. With communication possible again the Shuttle can tune in to the Tactical Air Navigation system, which will monitor the accuracy of the approach with a radio beam.

Mission Control 'Take TACAN. Energy and ground track look good to us.'

Commander 'Roger, TACAN acquisition and commencing third roll reversal.'

The speed brake is reduced to a 65% setting.

Mission Control 'Take air data.'

Pitot-static probes are deployed as a fourth and final S-turn brings the Shuttle across the coast of California at five times the speed of sound. Altitude is now 100,000ft. Speed is reducing rapidly and by the time the Terminal Area Energy Management Interface is reached (the point at which the line-up for the runway begins) the Shuttle is at 82,000ft (24,994m) and Mach 2.5.

As the spacecraft enters the Terminal Area Energy Management phase the yaw thrusters are de-activated and the Shuttle is now under full aerodynamic control like a normal aircraft. It has in effect become a glider, using carefully managed kinetic energy as well as ordinary lift to control the rate of descent.

Sonic booms echo across the desert as the 100-ton craft falls in a steep nose-down attitude, its approach specially timed so that the sun will not be in the eyes of the crew on the final leg. The Shuttle streaks across the bleak landmarks familiar to all Edwards test pilots: the small town of Bakersfield, then Tehachapi, then Mojave itself as the Base draws near.

Commander 'Waypoint One secured.'

This indicates that the Heading Alignment Circle has been reached, an imaginary cylinder in the sky of radius 20,000ft (6.096m), around which the Shuttle will fly to acquire the correct heading for the final approach to the runway. Workload on the flightdeck is now intense; with no power for an overshoot the landing has to be right first time.

The landing will be achieved under the direction of a Microwave Landing System similar to that used at an airport. Microwave beams are transmitted which feed reference data on the Shuttle's vertical and horizontal angle from the ideal approach path into the onboard computers, which then decide the appropriate instruction to give the digital autopilot.

As the Shuttle curves around the Heading Alignment Cylinder on to the final approach the surface wind direction and speed, together with the altimeter pressure setting, are transmitted to the Commander in the normal manner of air traffic control:

'Surface wind two zero zero, seven knots, set one zero zero niner.'

The runway looms large in the desert ahead. Beyond it, in the shimmering heat, lies the Wherry Housing area where the Commander once lived. Further in the distance is the flat expanse of Rosamond Dry Lake, the former landing ground of the X-15: the Captain of the Shuttle is too busy at this moment to remember the days when he flew F-104 chase planes for that pioneering rocket ship, but later, when the work is over, the thought may strike him. (Chase planes, in this case T-38 trainers, were used to chase the early Shuttle approaches, but this was discontinued as techniques were perfected.)

At 1,750ft (533m) a 'pre-flare' is conducted to establish a 1.5° glideslope (until now the angle has been 20°, compared with the normal 3° of an airliner approach). When the reduced angle is achieved the Shuttle is 135ft (41m) above the runway. At 90ft (27m) the landing gear is extended by a simple and irreversible gravity mechanism. Touchdown will follow in 15 seconds.

Commander 'Gear down and locked.'

A final flare reduces speed to 215mph (346km/hr) and the main wheels touch the runway.

The Orbiter continues its landing roll along the centreline for a full minute after the wheels hit. When the vehicle comes to rest it has used up 4,500ft (1,371m) with 15% use of brakes.

Mission Control 'We have wheels stopped.'

Still busy, the flight crew switch off the Auxiliary Power Units, de-activate the OMS and complete the post-landing checks. Mission Control informs the Commander that the landing has been nominal.

Mission Control 'No immediate post-landing deltas. Welcome home.'

Wearing protective clothing resembling space-suits (Self Contained Atmosphere Protection Ensemble Suits, SCAPES) technicians surround the vehicle, inspecting every crevice, noting areas of heavy scorching and other possible safety points.

Aboard the Shuttle the crew wait for the portable steps to be positioned so that they can leave the vehicle through the same hatch by which they entered a long week ago. Ahead lie the debriefings, the press conferences, the tours of manufacturers' plants and the lectures to schoolchildren which are all part of an astronaut's life. And beyond that, after more arduous training, medical checks and simulator sessions (so long as luck holds out), there will be another day, when a van will take them out through the Florida heat to the launch pad.

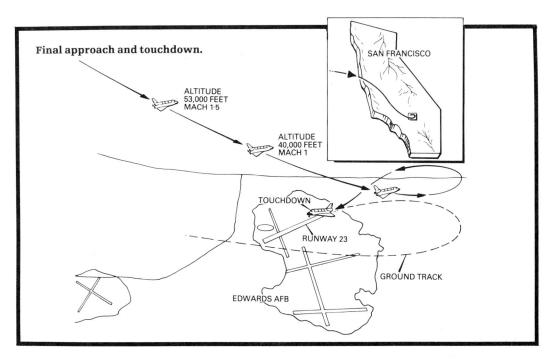

Final approach and touchdown.

ALTITUDE
53,000 FEET
MACH 1·5

ALTITUDE
40,000 FEET
MACH 1

SAN FRANCISCO

TOUCHDOWN

RUNWAY 23

GROUND TRACK

EDWARDS AFB

..Touchdown

THE FIRST 25 STS ORBITAL MISSIONS

KEY TO TERMS USED IN THIS TABLE:

Mission: Number of mission in sequence of successful Shuttle launches.
Designation: Original flight designation (which includes cancelled flights) and payload identification code.
Orbiter: Vehicle name and number of flight in sequence of successful flights by that vehicle.
Launch date: Date of successful launch.
Launch site: Number of pad and complex used.
Inclination: The angle between the plane of the Shuttle's orbit and the plane of the Earth's equator.
Altitude: Maximum altitude attained.
Landing date: Date of successful landing.
Landing site: Site, runway and complex used.
Orbits: Number of full orbits and (in the case of landings at Edwards Air Force Base) the number of the partial orbit during which landing occurred.
Duration: Flight time from lift-off to landing, calculated from SRB ignition until landing gear contact with runway; does not include SSME burn-time on pad or landing roll-out time.
Payloads: Mission number in operational flight sequence, major and secondary payloads, experiments and investigations, satellite deployment dates, etc.
Crew: Role designations of flight crew, Mission Specialists and Payload Specialists; also identifies RMS operators, EVA crew and MMU-trained astronauts. Note that EVA crew are designated for each mission regardless of whether an EVA is planned or not. In-flight shift teams are also identified. Unless otherwise indicated, crew members were NASA personnel.
Launch weight: 4,538,764lb (2,058,751kg) vehicle weight at SRB ignition.
EVA duration: Dates and 'total exposure' durations of each EVA, calculated from airlock depressurisation to repressurisation.
MMU flights: Full data on MMU operations.
Remarks: Summary of 'firsts', records, notable achievements, etc.

Mission: Shuttle 1
Designation: STS-1 (11A)
Orbiter: *Columbia* (OV-102) Flight 01
Launch date: 12 April 1981
Launch site: Launch complex 39 (Pad A) Kennedy Space Centre
Inclination: 40.3°

Maximum altitude: 166 statute miles (144 US nautical miles, 267km)
Landing date: 14 April 1981
Landing site: Runway 23 (Dry Lake Bed) Edwards Air Force Base
Orbits: 35, landing on 36
Duration: 2 days, 6 hours, 20 minutes, 52 seconds
Payload: *Orbital Flight Test (OFT) 1*
Office of Aeronautics & Space Technology (OAST)
  Orbiter Experiments Programme:
  (a) Aerodynamic Coefficient Identification Package
  (b) Development Flight Instrumentation (DFI)
Crew: Commander: John W. Young (EV1)
Pilot: Robert L. Crippen (EV2)
Launch weight: 4,501,284lb (2,041,751kg)
Remarks: First manned launch of Shuttle system, first manned flight of new vehicle not preceded by an unmanned flight, first manned flight by USA for nearly six years, first dry-land return of US manned spacecraft, first runway landing by any spacecraft (other than X-15). Opened 20th anniversary of manned spaceflight; Young's fifth mission (a world record)

Mission: Shuttle 2
Designation: STS-2 (21A)
Orbiter: *Columbia* (OV-102) Flight 02
Launch date: 12 November 1981
Launch site: LC 39 (Pad A) KSC
Inclination: 38°
Maximum altitude: 157 statute miles (136nm, 252.7km)
Landing date: 14 November 1981
Landing site: Runway 23 (DLB) Edwards AFB
Orbits: 35, landing on 36
Duration: 2 days, 6 hours, 13 minutes, 112 seconds
Payload: *OFT2*
Remote Manipulator System
Office of Space & Terrestrial Applications (OSTA-1):
  (a) Measurement of Air Pollution from Satellites (MAPS)
  (b) Shuttle Imaging Radar A (SIR-A)
  (c) Shuttle Multispectral Infra-Red Radiometer (SMIRR)
  (d) Feature Identification & Location Experiment
  (e) Ocean Colour Experiment
Induced Environment Contamination Monitor:
  (a) Mass Spectrometer
  (b) Camera/Photometer

(c) Cryogenic Quartz Crystal Monitor
(d) Temperature-Controlled Quartz Crystal Microbalance
(e) Optical Effects Module
(f) Passive Sample Array
(g) Cascade Impactor
(h) Air Sampler
(i) Dew Point Hygrometer
(j) Humidity Monitor
Day-Night Optical Survey of Lightning
Heflex Bio-engineering Test
Development Flight Instrumentation (DFI)
Crew: Commander: Joe H. Engle (EV1, RMS-trained)
Pilot: Richard H. Truly (EV2, RMS-trained)
Launch weight: Approx 4,475,943lb (2,030,243kg)
Remarks: First manned re-use of a spacecraft, first use of RMS, extensive experimentation package in payload bay. Mission shortened from planned five days due to faulty fuel cell discovered shortly after launch

---

Mission: Shuttle 3
Designation: STS-3 (21B)
Orbiter: *Columbia* (OV-102) Flight 03
Launch date: 22 March 1982
Launch site: LC 39 (Pad A) KSC
Inclination: 38°
Maximum altitude: 147 statute miles (127.7nm, 236.7km)
Landing date: 30 March 1982
Landing site: Runway 15, lake bed, Northrup Strip, White Sands Missile Range, New Mexico
Orbits: 128, landing on 129
Duration: 8 days, 0 hours, 4 minutes, 46 seconds
Payload: *OFT-3*
Remote Manipulator System
Office of Space Sciences (OSS-1)
(a) Contamination Monitor Package
(b) Micro-abrasion Foil Experiment
(c) Plant Growth Unit
(d) Plasma Diagnostics Package
(e) Shuttle-Spacelab Induced Atmosphere
(f) Solar Flare X-Ray Polarimeter
(g) Solar Ultra-Violet Spectral Irradiance Monitor
(h) Thermal Canister Experiment
(j) Vehicle Charging & Potential Experiment
Getaway Special Flight Verification Payload
Monodisperse Latex Reactor
Continuous Flow Electrophoresis System
Heflex Bio-engineering Test
Orbital Flight Test Pallet
Induced Environmental Contamination Monitor (IECM):
(a) Mass Spectrometer
(b) Camera/Photometer
(c) Cryogenic Quartz Crystal Microbalance
(d) Temperature-controlled Quartz Crystal Microbalance
(e) Optical Effects Module
(f) Passive Sample Array
(g) Cascade Impactor
(h) Air Sampler
(i) Dew Point Hygrometer
(j) Humidity Monitor

Shuttle Student Involvement Project:
(a) Insects in Flight Motion Study
OAST Orbital Experiments Programme:
(a) Aerodynamics Coefficient Identification Package (ACIP)
(b) Catalytic Surface Effects (CSE) Experiment
(c) Dynamic, Acoustic & Thermal Environment (DATE) Experiment
Development Flight Instrumentation
Crew: Commander: Jack R. Lousma (EV1, RMS-trained)
Pilot: Charles G. Fullerton (EV2, RMS-trained)
Launch weight: Approx 4,478,954lb (2,031,609kg)
Remarks: First extensive use of Orbiter as scientific platform, further use of RMS including first use to lift payload around cargo bay, first flight extension in flight, first landing at White Sands back-up recovery site

---

Mission: Shuttle 4
Designation: STS-4 (21C)
Orbiter: *Columbia* (OV-102) Flight 04
Launch date: 27 June 1982
Launch site: LC 39 (Pad A) KSC
Inclination: 28.5°
Maximum altitude: 197 statute miles (171nm, 317km)
Landing date: 4 July 1982
Landing site: Runway 22, concrete runway, Edwards AFB
Orbits: 112, landing on 113
Duration: 7 days, 1 hour, 9 minutes, 32 seconds
Payload: *OFT-4*
Remote Manipulator System (RMS)
Department of Defense (DoD 82-1):
(a) Ultraviolet Horizon Scanner (UHS)
(b) Cryogenic Infra-Red Radiance Instrument (CIRRIS)
Induced Environment Contamination Monitor (IECM):
(a) Mass Spectrometer
(b) Camera/Photometer
(c) Cryogenic Quartz Crystal Microbalance
(d) Optical Effects Module
(e) Passive Sample Array
(f) Cascade Impactor
(g) Air Sampler
(h) Dew Point Hygrometer
(i) Humidity Monitor
(j) Plasma Pressure Gauge
Monodisperse Latex Reactor
Night/Day Optical Survey of Lightning
CFES
Getaway Special (Utah State University):
(a) Fruit Fly Growth Experiment
(b) Brine Shrimp Growth Experiment
(c) Surface Tension Experiment
(d) Composite Curing Experiment
(e) Thermal Conductivity Experiment
(f) Microgravity Soldering Experiment
(g) Root Growth of Duckweed Experiment
(h) Homogeneous Alloy Experiment
(i) Algal Microgravity Bioassay Experiment

Shuttle Student Involvement Project:
  (a) Effects of Diet, Exercise and Zero-G on Lipoprotein Profiles
  (b) Effects of Space Travel on Levels of Trivalent Chromium in the Human Body
OAST Orbiter Experiments Programme:
  (a) Aerodynamic Coefficient Identification Package (ACIP)
  (b) Tile Gap Heating Effects (TGHE) Experiment
  (c) Catalytic Surface Effects (CSE) Experiment
  (d) Dynamic, Acoustic & Thermal Environment (DATE) Experiment
Development Flight Instrumentation
Crew: Commander: Thomas K. Mattingly II (EV1, RMS-trained)
Pilot: Henry W. Hartsfield Jr (EV2, RMS-trained)
Launch weight: Approx 4,482,888lb (2,033,393kg)
Remarks: Last test flight in OFT programme, first semi-dedicated DoD test mission, first in-flight test of donning/doffing EMU, continuation of Orbiter 'test bed' programme and use of RMS

Mission: Shuttle 5
Designation: STS-5 (31A)
Orbiter: *Columbia* (OV-102) Flight 05
Launch date: 11 November 1982
Launch site: LC39 (Pad A) KSC
Inclination: 28.5°
Maximum altitude: 184 statute miles (159.8nm, 296km)
Landing date: 16 November 1982
Landing site: Runway 22, Edwards AFB
Orbits: 81, landing on 82
Duration: 5 days, 2 hours, 14 minutes, 25 seconds
Payload: *Operational Flight 01*
Satellite Business Systems SBS-3/PAM-D (deployed Flight Day 1, 16 November)
Anik C3/PAM-D (deployed FD 2, 17 November)
EVA Task Simulation Device
Student Involvement Programme:
  (a) Growth of Ponefera in Zero-G
  (b) Convection in Zero-G
  (c) Formation of Crystals in Zero-G
Getaway Special:
  (a) X-Ray Radiation on Metallic Samples
OAST Orbiter Experiments Programme:
  (a) ACIP
  (b) TGHE
  (c) CSE
  (d) DATE
  (e) Atmospheric Luminosities Investigation (Glow) Experiment
  (f) Oxygen Atom Interaction with Materials Test
  (g) Development Flight Instrumentation
Crew: Commander: Vance D. Brand
Pilot: Robert F. Overmyer
MS1: William B. Lenoir (EV1)
MS2: Joseph P. Allen IV (EV2)
Launch weight: Approx 4,488,559lb (2,035,965kg)
Remarks: First operational mission in series, world's first four-person launch, first satellite deployments from Shuttle, first cancelled EVA from Shuttle, first flight of MS, first launch of US astronauts without launch-protection or escape system

---

Mission: Shuttle 6
Designation: STS-6 (31B)
Orbiter: *Challenger* (OV-099) Flight 01
Launch date: 4 April 1983
Launch site: LC 39 (Pad A) KSC
Inclination: 28.5°
Maximum altitude: 176.6 statute miles (153.4nm, 284.2km)
Landing date: 9 April 1983
Landing site: Runway 22 (concrete) Edwards AFB
Orbits: 80, landing on 81
Duration: 5 days, 0 hours, 23 minutes, 42 seconds
Payload: *Operational Flight 02*
TDRS-1/IUS and Support Structure (dep FD 1, 4 April)
EVA Task Simulation Device
CFES
Monodisperse Latex Reactor
Optical Survey of Lightning
Getaway Specials:
  (a) Artificial Snow Crystal Experiment
  (b) Seed Experiment
  (c) 'Scenic Fast'
  (d) Metal Beam Joiner
  (e) Metal Alloy
  (f) Foam Metal
  (g) Metal Purification
  (h) Electroplating
  (i) Microbiology
Crew: Commander: Paul J. Weitz
Pilot: Karol J. Bobko
MS1: Story F. Musgrave (EV1)
MS2: Donald H. Peterson (EV2)
Launch weight: Approx 4,490,498lb (2,036,845kg)
EVA duration: EVA-1, 7 April=4 hours, 17 minutes
Remarks: First flight of *Challenger*, first launch of IUS upper stage, first Shuttle EVA

Mission: Shuttle 7
Designation: STS-7 (31C)
Orbiter: *Challenger* (OV-009) Flight 02
Launch date: 18 June 1983
Launch site: LC 39 (Pad A) KSC
Inclination: 28.45°
Maximum altitude: 195 statute miles (169.3nm, 313.8km)
Landing date: 24 June 1983
Landing site: Runway 15 (DLB) Edwards AFB
Orbits: 97, landing on 98
Duration: 6 days, 2 hours, 23 minutes, 59 seconds
Payload: *Operational Flight 03*
RMS
Anik C2/PAM-D (dep FD 1, 18 June)
Palapa B/PAM-D (dep FD 2, 19 June)
Shuttle Pallet Satellite (dep/retrieved FD 5, 22 June)
OSTA-2:
  (a) Materials Experiment Assembly (MEA)
  (b) Vapour Growth of Alloy-Type Semi-Conductor Crystals
  (c) Liquid Phase Miscibility Gap Materials
  (d) Continuous Processing of Glass-Forming Materials
MAUS:
  (a) Three German GAS materials experiments
Mission-Peculiar Equipment Support Structure (to hold OSTA-2)

Monodisperse Latex Reactor Experiment
CFES
Getaway Specials:
  (a) Five German Students Experiments
  (b) Three Purdue University
  (c) Two California Institute of Technology
  (d) Camden and Wilson High Schools Experiments
      (sponsored by RCA, live ant colony in Zero-G)
  (e) Nine Edsyn Inc
  (f) One Goddard Space Flight Center
  (g) One USAF/NRL
OAST Orbiter Experiments Programme:
  (a) ACIP
  (b) High Resolution Accelerometer Package
Crew: Commander: Robert L. Crippen
Pilot: Frederick H. Hauck
MS1: John M. Fabian (EV1, RMS-trained)
MS2: Sally K. Ride (RMS-trained)
MS3: Norman E. Thagard (EV2)
Launch weight: Approx 4,485,579lb (2,034,614kg)
Remarks: First five-person launch, first US woman
in space, first astronaut (Crippen) to make a second
Shuttle flight and also first to fly in more than one
Orbiter vehicle, first flight of Group 8 astronaut
intake, first deployment and capture of payload by
RMS and thus enabling first photographs showing
full view of Orbiter in space

Mission: Shuttle 8
Designation: STS-8 (31D)
Orbiter: *Challenger* (OV-099) Flight 03
Launch date: 30 August 1983
Launch site: LC 39 (Pad A) KSC
Inclination: 28.45°
Maximum altitude: 191 statute miles (165.9nm,
307.4km)
Landing date: 5 September 1984
Landing site: Runway 22 (concrete) Edwards AFB
Orbits: 96, landing on 97
Duration: 6 days, 1 hour, 8 minutes, 40 seconds
Payload: *Operational Flight 04*
RMS
Insat M1B/PAM-D (dep FD 2, 31 August)
Payload Flight Test Article
US Postal Service philatelic covers (in eight GAS
  canisters and two boxes in DFI pallet)
CFES
Development Flight Instrumentation Pallet
Shuttle Student Involvement Programme
  Experiment
Animal Enclosure Module (eight rats)
Getaway Specials:
  (a) Cosmic Ray Upset Experiment
  (b) Ultraviolet-sensitive Photographic Emulsion
      Experiment
  (c) Snow Crystal Experiment
  (d) Contamination Monitor Package
Crew: Commander: Richard H. Truly (EV1,
RMS-trained)
Pilot: Daniel C. Brandenstein
MS1: Dale A. Gardner (EV2, RMS-trained)
MS2: Guion S. Bluford
MS3: William E. Thornton
Launch weight: Approx 4,493,007lb (2,037,983kg)

Remarks: First night launch and night landing of
STS, first flight of black American, near disaster at
launch when SRB casing almost burned through,
Thornton became oldest man to fly in space (54)

Mission: Shuttle 9
Designation: STS-9 (41A) Spacelab 1
Orbiter: *Columbia* (OV-102) Flight 06
Launch date: 28 November 1983
Launch site: LC 39 (Pad A) KSC
Inclination: 57°
Maximum altitude: 135 statute miles (117.3nm,
217.3km)
Landing date: 8 December 1983
Landing site: Runway 17, Edwards AFB
Orbits: 166, landing on 167
Duration: 10 days, 7 hours, 47 minutes, 23 seconds
Payload: *Operational Flight 05*
Spacelab 1 (Long Module & Single Pallet):
  (a) Six Astronomy and Solar Physics Experiments
  (b) Six Space Plasma Physics Experiments
  (c) Six Atmospheric Physics and Earth
      Observation Experiments
  (d) 16 Life Sciences Experiments
  (e) 36 Materials Sciences Experiments
Crew: Commander: John W. Young (EV1, Red Shift
Leader/Pilot)
Pilot: Brewster H. Shaw Jr (Blue Shift Leader/Pilot)
MS1: Owen K. Garriott (EV2, Blue MS)
MS2: Robert A. Parker (Red MS)
PS1: Byron K. Lichtenberg, MIT (Blue PS)
PS2: Ulf Merbold, ESA (Red PS)
Launch weight: Approx 4,503,095lb (2,042,559kg)
Remarks: First flight of European Space Agency
(ESA) Spacelab Mission Module, first flight of
Payload Specialist (PS), first six-person launch, first
US launch of a non-American (Merbold, the first
West German in space), first non-NASA or non-
military US astronaut (Lichtenberg), first 24-hour
shift system, heaviest STS launch to date, longest
STS flight to date, Young first astronaut to fly a sixth
mission (two on Gemini, two on Apollo, two on STS)

Mission: Shuttle 10
Designation: STS-11 (41B)
Orbiter: *Challenger* (OV-099) Flight 04
Launch date: 3 February 1984
Launch site: LC 39 (Pad A) KSC
Inclination: 28.5°
Maximum altitude: 165 statute miles (143.3nm,
265.5km)
Landing date: 11 February 1984
Landing site: Runway 33, KSC
Orbits: 127
Duration: 7 days, 23 hours 15 minutes, 55 seconds
Payload: *Operational Flight 06*
RMS
Two manned Manoeuvering Units (Nos 2 and 3)
MMU Flight Support Structures
Palapa B2/PAM-D (dep FD1, 3 February)
Westar 6/PAM-D (dep FD4, 6 February)
Integrated Rendezvous Target (IRT) (dep FD 3,
  5 February)
Shuttle Student Involvement Programme:
  (a) Animal Enclosure Module (six rats)

Getaway Specials:
  (a) Utah State University/University of Aberdeen; AIAA (Utah section)
  (b) Atomic Oxygen Flux Monitor
  (c) Arc Lamp research
  (d) Cosmic Ray Upset Experiment
Two Cinema-360 Cameras
Monodisperse Latex Reactor
Acoustic Containerless Experiment System
Ion Electric Focussing Experiment
Crew: Commander: Vance D. Brand
Pilot: Robert L. Gibson
MS1: Robert L. Stewart (EV2, MMU-trained)
MS2: Bruce McCandless II (EV1, MMU-trained)
MS3: Ronald E. McNair (RMS-trained)
Launch weight: Approx 4,504,350lb (2,043,128kg)
EVA duration: EVA-1, 7 February=5 hours, 55 minutes
EVA-2, 9 February=6 hours, 17 minutes
Total=12 hours, 12 minutes
MMU flights: Unit 2=Two flights, total 1 hour, 31 minutes
Unit 3=Three flights, total 3 hours, 39 minutes
Total MMU time=5 hours, 10 minutes in five flights
Remarks: First use of MMU in free flight, first landing at KSC. Both commerical satellites successfully deployed but failed to reach planned orbits due to faulty PAM stages. IRT balloon exploded shortly after deployment but crew tracked the larger particles successfully

Mission: Shuttle 11
Designation: STS-13 (41C)
Orbiter: *Challenger* (OV-099) Flight 05
Launch date: 6 April 1984
Launch site: LC 39 (Pad A) KSC
Inclination: 28.5°
Maximum altitude: 290 statute miles (251.8nm, 466.7km)
Landing date: 13 April 1984
Landing site: Runway 17, Edwards AFB
Orbits: 106, landing on 107
Duration: 6 days, 23 hours, 40 minutes 5 seconds
Payload: *Operational Flight 07*
RMS
Two MMUs (Nos 2 and 3)+Flight Support Structures
Lond Duration Exposure Facility (LDEF) (dep FD 2, 7 April)
Fixed Service Structure
Shuttle Student Involvement Programme:
  (a) Study of 3,000 honey bees in Zero-G
IMAX Camera
Cinema-360 Camera
Crew: Commander: Robert L. Crippen
Pilot: Francis R. Scobee
MS1: Terry J. Hart (RMS-trained)
MS2: George D. Nelson, NASA (EV1, MMU-trained)
MS3: James D. van Hoften, NASA (EV2, MMU-trained)
Launch weight: 4,538,764lb (2,058,751kg)
EVA duration: EVA-1, 8 April=2 hours 57 minutes
EVA-2, 11 April=6 hours, 16 minutes
Total=9 hours, 13 minutes
MMU flights: Unit 2=One flight, total 42 minutes
Unit 3=One flight, total 28 minutes

Total MMU time=1 hour, 10 minutes in two flights
Remarks: First direct ascent into orbit, first LDEF deployment, first *operational* use of MMU, first retrieval, repair and redeployment of satellite in orbit ('Solar Max')

Mission: Shuttle 12
Designation: STS-14 (41-D)
Orbiter: *Discovery* (OV-103) Flight 01
Launch date: 30 August 1984
Launch site: LC 39 (Pad A) KSC
Inclination: 28.45°
Maximum altitude: 173 statute miles (150.2nm, 278.4km)
Landing date: 5 September 1984
Landing site: Runway 17, Edwards AFB
Orbits: 96, landing on 97
Duration: 6 days, 0 hours, 56 minutes, 4 seconds
Payload: *Operational Flight 08*
RMS
SBS-4 (dep FD 1, 30 August)
Leasat 1 (dep FD 2, 31 August)
Telstar 3C (dep FD 3, 1 September)
OAST-1:
  (a) Solar Array Experiment
  (b) Dynamic Augmentation Experiment
  (c) Solar Cell Calibration Facility
CFES
IMAX
Radiation Monitoring Experiment
Shuttle Student Involvement Experiment
CLOUDS
Crew: Commander: Henry W. Hartsfield (RMS-trained)
Pilot: Michael L. Coats
MS1: Richard A. Mullane (EV1)
MS2: Judith A. Resnik (RMS-trained)
MS3: Steven A. Hawley (EV2)
PS1: Charles D. Walker, McDonnell-Douglas
Launch weight: 4,501,284lb (2,041,751kg)
Remarks: First flight of *Discovery* (following the first Shuttle launch pad abort in June), first triple satellite launch using PAM, first flight of Solar 'Wing' array, first flight of an astronaut from private industry (Walker). RMS was used to dislodge icicle from waste outlet near end of mission; if unsuccessful an EVA would have been necessary

Mission: Shuttle 13
Designation: STS-17 (41G)
Orbiter: *Challenger* (OV-099) Flight 06
Launch date: 5 October 1984
Launch site: LC 39 (Pad A) KSC
Inclination: 57°
Maximum altitude: 218 statute miles (189.3nm, 350.8km)
Landing date: 13 October 1984
Landing site: Runway 33 KSC
Orbits: 133
Duration: 8 days, 5 hours, 23 minutes 33 seconds
Payload: *Operational Flight 09*
OSTA-3:
  (a) Shuttle Imaging Radar B (SIR-B)
  (b) Large Format Camera

(c) Measurement of Air Pollution from Satellites (MAPS)
(d) Feature Identification & Location Experiment (FILE)
Earth Radiation Budget Experiment:
(a) ERB Satellite (dep FD 1, 5 October, by RMS)
(b) ERB non-scanner
(c) Stratospheric Aerosol & Gas Experiment (SAGE-2)
Orbital Refuelling System (ORS)
Canadian Experiments (CANEX):
(a) NRC Space Vision System
(b) Advanced Composite Materials Exposure
(c) Sun Photometer measurements
(d) Atmospheric Emission and Shuttle Glow Measurements
(e) Space Adaptation Syndrome Experiment Studies
Eight Getaway Specials
Radiation Monitoring Equipment
Thermaluminescent Dosimeter (TLD)
RMS
Crew: Commander: Robert L. Crippen
Pilot: Jon A. McBride
MS1: Sally K. Ride (RMS-trained)
MS2: Kathryn D. Sullivan (EV2)
MS3: David C. Leestma (EV1)
PS1: Marc Garneau, NRC of Canada
PS2: Paul Scully-Power, civilian employed by USN
Launch weight: 4,499,000lb (2,040,701kg)
EVA duration: EVA-1, 11 October=3 hours, 27 minutes
Remarks: First seven-person crew, first US woman EVA, first flight of two women together, first US woman to fly twice (Ride), first Group 9 astronaut to fly, (Leestma), highest orbital altitude yet attained by STS, first demonstration of manually-operated refuelling technique, first Canadian in space, first Australian-born astronaut (Scully-Power), first astronaut to fly four shuttle missions (Crippen)

Mission: Shuttle 14
Designation: STS-19 (51A)
Orbiter: *Discovery* (OV-103) Flight 02
Launch date: 8 November 1984
Launch site: LC 39 (Pad A) KSC
Inclination: 28.5°
Maximum altitude: 220 statute miles (191nm, 354km)
Landing date: 16 November 1984
Landing site: Runway 15, KSC
Orbits: 127
Duration: 7 days, 23 hours, 44 minutes, 56 seconds
Payload: *Operational Flight 10*
RMS
Anik D2(Telesat)/PAM-D (dep FD 2, 9 November)
Leasat (Syncom 4) (dep FD 3, 10 November)
Westar 6 Retrieval Pallet
Palapa B2 Retrieval Pallet
Radiation Monitoring Equipment
Diffusive Mixing of Organic Solutions
Two MMUs (Nos 2 and 3)+Flight Support Structures
Two 'Stinger' satellite capture devices
Crew: Commander: Frederick H. Hauck (RMS-trained)

Pilot: David M. Walker
MS1: Joseph P. Allen IV (EV1, MMU-trained)
MS2: Anna L. Fisher (RMS-trained)
MS3: Dale A. Gardner, NASA (EV2, MMU-trained)
Launch weight: 4,518,761lb (2,049,665kg)
EVA durations: EVA-1, 12 November=6 hours, 0 minutes
EVA-2: 14 November=5 hours, 42 minutes
Total=11 hours, 42 minutes
MMU duration: Unit 2=One flight, 1 hour 40 minutes
Unit 3=One flight, 2 hours, 22 minutes
Total MMU time=4 hours, 2 minutes in two flights
Remarks: Retrieved stranded satellites deployed from Shuttle 10 in February 1984: Palapa B2 retrieved FD 5 (12 November), Westar 6 retrieved FD 7 (14 November), Fisher the first mother to fly in space

Mission: Shuttle 15
Designation: STS-20 (51C)
Orbiter: *Discovery* (OV-103) Flight 3
Launch date: 24 January 1985
Launch site: LC 39 (Pad A) KSC
Inclination: Not available for publication
Maximum altitude: Not available for publication
Landing date: 27 January 1985
Landing site: Runway 15, KSC
Orbits: 48
Duration: 3 days, 1 hour, 33 minutes, 13 seconds
Payload: *Operational Flight 11 (DoD-Dedicated Shuttle Flight 01)*
GEO military electronic monitoring satellite/IUS (date of deployment not available for publication)
Blood Flow Experiment
Crew: Commander: Thomas K. Mattingly II
Pilot: Loren J. Shriver
MS1: Ellison Onizuka (EV1)
MS2: James F. Buchli (EV2)
PS1: Gary E. Payton, USAF MSE
Launch weight: Not available for publication
Remarks: First dedicated-DoD Shuttle mission, first fully secret US manned flight, first flight of USAF MSE as PS, first oriental American in space. Despite secrecy of launch weight, weight at orbital insertion known to be 250,891lb (1,138,017kg)

Mission: Shuttle 16
Designation: STS-23 (51D)
Orbiter: *Discovery* (OV-103) Flight 04
Launch date: 12 April 1985
Launch site: LC 39 (Pad A) KSC
Inclination: 28.5°
Maximum altitude: 324 statute miles (281nm, 521km)
Landing date: 17 April 1985
Landing site: Runway 33, KSC
Orbits: 110
Duration: 6 days, 23 hours, 55 minutes, 23 seconds
Payload: *Operational Flight 12*
RMS
Telesat 1 (Anik C1)/PAM-D (dep FD 1, 12 April)
Syncom IV-3 (Leasat 3) (dep FD 2, 13 April)

American Flight Echocardiograph (AFE)
CFES
Student Experiments:
  (a) Statoliths in Corn Root Caps
  (b) Effects of Weightlessness on Ageing Brain
      Cells
Getaway Specials:
  (a) Capillary Pump Loop (CPL)
  (b) Physics of Solids and Liquids in Zero-G
Educational Experiments (Toys in Space)
Protein Crystal Growth Experiments
Phase Positioning Experiments
Astronomy Photography Verification Experiment
Crew: Commander: Karol J. Bobko
Pilot: Donald E. Williams
MS1: Margaret R. Seddon (RMS-trained)
MS2: Jeffrey A. Hoffman (EV1, RMS-trained)
MS3: S. David Griggs (EV2)
PS1: Charles D. Walker, McDonnell-Douglas
PS2: E. Jake Garn, US Senate
Launch weight: 4,504,882lb (2,043,369kg)
EVA duration: EVA-1, 16 April=3 hours, 0 minutes
Remarks: Despite successful deployment of
  Leasat 3, satellite did not activate as planned and
  a contingency EVA was performed to attempt a
  rescue with RMS. This failed. First flight of US
  Senator, first PS to fly twice (Walker, who had
  more space-time experience than whole crew).
  Brake failure and burst tyre on landing (no
  hazard)

Mission: Shuttle 17
Designation: STS-24 (51B) Spacelab 3
Orbiter: *Challenger* (OV-099) Flight 07
Launch date: 29 April 1985
Launch site: LC 39 (Pad A) KSC
Inclination: 57°
Maximum altitude: 324 statute miles (281nm,
521km)
Landing date: 6 May 1985
Landing site: Runway 17, Edwards AFB
Orbits: 108, landing on 109
Duration: 7 days, 0 hours, 8 minutes, 50 seconds
Payload: *Operational Flight 13*
Spacelab 3 (Long Module & Special Support Pallet):
  (a) Three Materials Science Experiments
  (b) Four Life Sciences Experiments
  (c) Two Fluid Mechanics Experiments
  (d) Four Atmospherics/Astronomical Experiments
Two Getaway Special canisters containing:
  (a) Nusat satellite
  (b) GLOMR satellite
Crew: Commander: Robert F. Overmyer (Gold
Leader/Pilot)
Pilot: Frederick D. Gregory, NASA (EV1, Silver
Leader/Pilot)
MS1: Don L. Lind (Gold MS)
MS2: Norman E. Thagard (EV2, Silver MS)
MS3: William E. Thornton (Gold MS)
PS1: Taylor Wang, JPL (Gold PS, fluids)
PS2: Lodewijk van den Berg, EG&G Corp (Silver PS,
materials)
Launch weight: 4,501,581lb (2,041, 872kg)
Remarks: The third designated Spacelab became
the second in flight sequence due to re-scheduling.

Trouble-free mission apart from failure of GLOMR
satellite deployment and leakage of feed from
Animal Holding Facility. Troubleshooting by Wang
saved his experiment. Crew included three members
of age 50+; Don Lind, the first Mormon in space, had
waited over 19 years to make his first flight

Mission: Shuttle 18
Designation: STS-25 (51G)
Orbiter: *Discovery* (OV-13) Flight 05
Launch date: 17 June 1985
Launch site: LC 39 (Pad A) KSC
Inclination: 28.45°
Maximum altitude: 253.3 statute miles (220nm,
407.7km)
Landing date: 24 June 1985
Landing site: Runway 23, Edwards AFB
Orbits: 111, landing on 112
Duration: 7 days, 1 hour, 38 minutes, 58 seconds
Payload: *Operational Flight 14*
RMS
Morelos A/PAM-D (dep FD 1, 17 June)
Arabsat 1B/PAM-D (dep FD 2, 18 June)
Telstar 3D/PAM-D (dep FD 3, 19 June)
Spartan 1 (dep FD 4, 20 June, retrieved FD 6, 22 June,
  by RMS)
Automatic Directional Solidification Furnace
French Echocardiograph Experiment
French Postural Experiment
High Precision Tracking Experiment
Arab Scientific Experiments
Getaway Specials:
  (a) Liquid Sloshing Behaviour in Microgravity
  (b) Slipcasting under Microgravity Conditions
  (c) Fundamental Studies of Manganese-Bismuth
  (d) 12 Texas Students' Experiments
  (e) Space Ultraviolet Radiation Experiment
  (f) Capillary Pump Loop
Crew: Commander: Daniel C. Brandenstein
Pilot: John O. Creighton
MS1: Steven R. Nagel (EV2)
MS2: John M. Fabian (EV1, RMS-trained)
MS3: Shannon W. Lucid (RMS-trained)
PS1: Prince Sultan Salman Abdul Aziz Al-Saud (Saudi
Arabia)
PS2: Patrick Baudry, CNES (France)
Launch weight: 4,515,043lb (2,047,978kg)
Remarks: Laser tracking experiment failed in early
attempts due to Shuttle positioning error. First Arab
in space (Al-Saud, also first Royal in space), first
Frenchman to fly with US (Baudry, whose flight also
made France the only country to have flown its
nationals with both USA and USSR), oldest woman in
space (Lucid at 42)

Mission: Shuttle 19
Designation: STS-26 (51F) Spacelab 2
Orbiter: *Challenger* (OV-099) Flight 8
Launch date: 29 July 1985
Launch site: LC 39 (Pad A) KSC
Inclination: 49.5°
Maximum altitude: 195.8 statute miles (170nm,
315km)
Landing date: 5 August 1985
Landing site: Runway 23, Edwards AFB

Orbits: 125, landing on 126
Duration: 7 days, 22 hours, 45 minutes, 27 seconds
Payload: *Operational Flight 15*
Spacelab 2 (three Pallets+'Igloo'):
  (a) Three Solar Physics Experiments
  (b) One Astrophysics Experiment
  (c) Three Plasma Physics Experiments
  (d) Two High-Energy Astrophysics Experiments
  (e) One Infra-Red Astronomy Experiment
  (f) One Technology Research Experiment
  (g) Two Life Sciences Experiments
  (h) Four additional minor experiments
RMS
Crew: Commander: Charles G. Fullerton (Red/Blue Shift Supervisor)
Pilot: Roy D. Bridges (Red Leader/Pilot)
MS1: Karl G. Henize (Red MS)
MS2: Story F. Musgrave (Blue Leader/Pilot, (EV1)
MS3: Anthony W. England (Blue MS, EV2)
PS1: Loren W. Acton, Lockheed (Red PS)
PS2: John-David Bartoe, civilian employed by USN (Blue PS)
Launch weight: 4,514,504lb (2,047,734kg)
Remarks: PDP released FD 3, 31 July, retrieved same day. First Abort to Orbit (ATO) of STS programme, mission continued successfully in lower-than-planned orbit. Carbonated drinks tested in space, Henize becomes oldest man to fly (58), England first man to fly in space after resigning from NASA (in 1972, re-employed 1979). This mission followed the second STS launch pad abort

---

Mission: Shuttle 20
Designation: STS-27 (51I)
Orbiter: *Discovery* (OV-103) Flight 06
Launch date: 27 August 1985
Launch site: LC 39 (Pad A) KSC
Inclination: 28.45°
Maximum altitude: 317.8 statute miles (276nm, 511.5km)
Landing date: 3 September 1985
Landing site: Runway 23, Edwards AFB
Orbits: 111 landing on 112
Duration: 7 days, 2 hours, 17 minutes, 42 seconds
Payload: *Operational Flight 16*
RMS
ASC-1/PAM-D (dep FD 1, 27 August, after Aussat 1)
Aussat 1/PAM-D (dep FD 1, 27 August)
Syncom IV-4 (Leasat 4) (dep FD 3, 29 August)
Leasat 3 Repair Equipment
Physical Vapour Transportation of Organic Solids Experiment
Crew: Commander: Joe H. Engle
Pilot: Richard O. Covey
MS1: Mike Lounge (RMS-trained)
MS2: James van Hoften, NASA (EV1, RMS-trained)
MS3: William F. Fisher, NASA (EV2)
Launch weight: 4,518,803lb (2,049,684kg)
EVA durations: EVA-1, 31 August=7 hours, 8 minutes
EVA-2, 1 September=4 hours, 26 minutes
Total=11 hours, 34 minutes
Remarks: Dramatic in-flight repair of Leasat 3 (abandoned by Shuttle 16 crew in April 1985) successful, van Hoften becomes Shuttle EVA

duration record holder (20 hours, 47 minutes, including 28 minutes MMU, totalled from Shuttles 11 and 20)

Mission: Shuttle 21
Designation: STS-28 (51J)
Orbiter: *Atlantis* (OV-104) Flight 01
Launch date: 3 October 1985
Launch site: LC 39 (Pad A) KSC
Inclination: 28.52°
Maximum altitude: 368.5 statute miles (320nm, 593km)
Landing date: 7 October 1985
Landing site: Runway 23, Edwards AFB
Orbits: Not available for publication
Duration: 4 days, 1 hour, 45 minutes, 30 seconds
Payload: *Operational Flight 17 (Dedicated DoD Shuttle Flight 02)*
Two DSCS-3 Military Communications Satellites/ Single IUS
NASA Bios Mid Deck Experiment
Crew: Commander Karol J. Bobko
Pilot: Ronald J. Grabe
MS1: David Hilmers (EV2)
MS2: Robert Stewart (EV1)
PS: William Pailes, USAF (MSE)
Launch weight: Not available for publication
Remarks: First flight of *Atlantis*, second MSE identified, highest Shuttle altitude to date, Bobko makes second flight in 136 days, his third overall. Second dedicated DoD mission

---

Mission: Shuttle 22
Designation: STS-30 (61A) Spacelab D1
Orbiter: *Challenger* (OV-099) Flight 09
Launch date: 30 October 1985
Launch site: LC 39 (Pad A) KSC
Inclination: 57°
Maximum altitude: 230.3 statute miles (200nm, 370.6km)
Landing date: 6 November 1985
Landing site: Runway 17, Edwards AFB
Orbits: 111 landing on 112
Duration: 7 days, 0 hours, 44 minutes, 51 seconds
Payload: *Operational Flight 18*
Spacelab D1 (Long Module):
  (a) 17 Fluid Physics Experiments
  (b) 31 Solidification Experiments
  (c) 17 Biological Experiments
  (d) Five Medical Experiments
  (e) Six Space-Time Interaction Experiments
GLOMR in GAS container (dep FD 1, 30 October)
Special Pallet, holding:
  (a) Navex Experiments
  (b) Materials Experiments Assembly
Crew: Commander: Henry W. Hartsfield (Red/Blue Co-ordinator)
Pilot: Steven R. Nagel (Blue Leader/Pilot, EV1)
MS1: Bonnie J. Dunbar, (Blue MS)
MS2: James F. Buchli (Red Leader/Pilot, EV2)
MS3: Guion S. Bluford Jr (Red MS)
PS1: Ernst Messerschmid, DFVLR (Red)
PS2: Reinhard Furrer, DFVLR (Blue)
PS3: Wubbo J. Ockels, ESA (not assigned team)
Launch weight: 4,504,741lb (2,043,305kg)

Remarks: First eight-person launch, first US mission to be partly controlled from outside USA, first flight to carry more than one national of a country other than USA or USSR (Messerschmid and Furrer both West Germans, Ockels a Dutch citizen). Nagel set record of only 128 days between missions

Mission: Shuttle 23
Designation: STS-31 (61B)
Orbiter: *Atlantis* (OV-104) Flight 02
Launch date: 26 November 1985
Launch site: LC 39 (Pad A) KSC
Inclination: 28.5°
Maximum altitude: 218.8 statute miles (190nm, 352.1km)
Landing date: 3 December 1985
Landing site: Runway 22, Edwards AFB
Orbits: 108, landing on 109
Duration: 6 days 21 hours, 4 minutes, 49 seconds
Payload: *Operational Flight 19*
RMS
Morelos/PAM-D (dep FD 1, 26 November)
Aussat-2/PAM-D (dep FD 2, 27 November)
Satcom KU-2/PAM-D2 (dep FD 3, 28 November)
Experimental Assembly of Structures with EVA (EASE)
Assembly Concept for Construction of Erectable Space Structure (ACCESS)
IMAX Camera
Getaway Special (Telesat Canada)
CFES
Diffusion Mixing of Organic Solution (DMOS)
Morelos Payload Specialist Experiments
Protein Characterization
Crew: Commander: Brewster H. Shaw Jr
Pilot: Bryan O'Connor
MS1: Sherwood Spring (EV2)
MS2: Mary L. Cleave (RMS-trained)
MS3: Jerry L. Ross (EV1)
PS1: Charles D. Walker, McDonnell-Douglas
PS2: Rudolfo Neri Vela, Mexico
Launch weight: 4,518,601lb (2,049,592kg)
EVA durations: EVA-1, 29 November=5 hours, 30 minutes
EVA-2, 1 December=6 hours, 30 minutes
Total=12 hours
Remarks: First flight of Mexican astronaut, second night launch of STS, first use of PAM-D2 upper stage, first construction in space, Walker becomes first PS to make a third flight (ending the mission with more Shuttle experience than any NASA astronaut except Crippen and Hartsfield)

Mission: Shuttle 24
Designation: STS-32 (61C)
Orbiter: *Columbia* (OV-102) Flight 07
Launch date: 12 January 1986
Launch site: LC 39 (Pad A) KSC
Inclination: 28.5°
Maximum altitude: 201.5 statute miles (175nm, 324.3km)
Landing date: 18 January 1986
Landing site: Runway 22, Edwards AFB
Orbits: 96, landing on 97

Duration: 6 days, 2 hours, 4 minutes, 9 seconds
Payload: *Operational Flight 20*
Satcom K-1/PAM-D2 (dep FD 1, 18 January)
Hitch-hiker G1
13 GAS canisters
Infra-Red Imaging Experiment (IR-IE)
Materials Science Laboratory (MSL-2)
Initial Blood Storage Experiment (IBSE)
Comet Halley Active Monitoring Programme (CHAMP)
Three Student Experiments (SSIP)
University of Alabama Cancer Experiment
NASA Video for US/Latin America select video
Crew: Commander: Robert L. Gibson
Pilot: Charles F. Bolden Jr
MS1: George D. Nelson (EV1)
MS2: Steven A. Hawley
MS3: Franklin R. Chiang-Diaz (EV2)
PS1: Robert J. Cenker, RCA
PS2: William Nelson, US House of Representatives
Launch weight: 4,516,472lb (2,048,627kg)
Remarks: Record eight attempts at launch and three at de-orbit. Second politician in space, first Latin American NASA astronaut, first flight of *Columbia* for two years, maximum number of Getaway Specials on one flight (using bridge across payload bay), first flight of two namesakes(!). Launch delays meant that Hawley had made six rides to the launch pad to achieve two flights

Mission: Shuttle 25
Designation: STS-33 (51L)
Orbiter: *Challenger* (OV-099) Flight 10
Launch date: 28 January 1986
Launch site: LC 39 (Pad B) KSC
Inclination: 28.5°
Maximum altitude: Planned 176 statute miles (153nm, 283.5km)
Landing date: Planned 3 February 1986
Landing site: Planned Runway 33, KSC
Orbits: Planned 97
Duration: Planned 6 days, 34 minutes
Payload: *Operational Flight 21*
TDRS-B/IUS+Support Structure
Spartan-Halley
Teacher in Space Project
CHAMP
Fluid Dynamics Experiment
Phase Partitioning Experiment
Radiation Monitoring Experiment
Three Student Experiments
Crew: Commander: Francis R. Scobee
Pilot: Michael J. Smith
MS1: Judith A. Resnik
MS2: Ellison S. Onizuka (EV1)
MS3: Ronald E. McNair (EV2)
PS1: Gregory Jarvis, Hughes Aircraft Corporation
PS2: Sharon Christa McAuliffe, Teacher
Launch weight: 4,529,122lb (2,054,364kg)
Remarks: First STS launch from Pad 39B. *Challenger* broke up due to aerodynamic forces following in-flight explosion 73 seconds after launch. No survivors